A. Judd (Ansel Judd) Northrup

Camps and Tramps in the Adirondacks, and grayling fishing in northern Michigan

A Record of Summer Vacations in the Wilderness

A. Judd (Ansel Judd) Northrup

Camps and Tramps in the Adirondacks, and grayling fishing in northern Michigan
A Record of Summer Vacations in the Wilderness

ISBN/EAN: 9783337178857

Printed in Europe, USA, Canada, Australia, Japan

Cover: Foto ©ninafisch / pixelio.de

More available books at **www.hansebooks.com**

CAMPS AND TRAMPS

IN THE

ADIRONDACKS,

AND

GRAYLING FISHING IN NORTHERN MICHIGAN:

A RECORD OF

Summer Vacations in the Wilderness.

BY

A. JUDD NORTHRUP.

SYRACUSE, N. Y.:
DAVIS, BARDEEN & CO., PUBLISHERS.
NEW YORK: BAKER, PRATT & CO.

1880.

COPYRIGHT, 1880.

By A. JUDD NORTHRUP.

PREFACE.

The incidents recorded in the following pages have been neither invented nor exaggerated to any appreciable degree. I have written in the belief that the actual doings of real personages, always and everywhere, have an interest of themselves quite independent of the manner of the telling, if the telling be truthful. So much I meant to be sure of at all hazards. What we said, also, is perhaps as veraciously set forth as the average interviewer reports his unwilling victim. I have endeavored, indeed to give to the reader truthful pictures of the actual summer vacation life in the Adirondacks, to refresh the recollection of those who have camped and tramped where we did, and to bring back somewhat of their enjoyment of the lakes and mountains and streams; and also to give to others who may read these records a reasonable, vivid and fair impression of the wilderness and the experiences of summer life there.

The chapters on Grayling Fishing have been added, as having at least a cousinly relationship to the general subject of the book.

The wisest of men, off in the woods, on a summer vacation, are "boys out of school;" and they seldom carry much of the "shop" with them from office, store or desk. The personages who appear in the following pages are no exception to the rule. Doubtless they could have talked any amount of philosophy, law, poetry, and wisdom of all sorts; but, indisputably, they did not. Indeed, I do not think the reader who has selected this book, from its title, for a leisure hour by the fireside or under the trees, is looking between these covers for that kind of thing. I hope rather to meet his expectation that here is something of the woods woodsy, of the camp merry, of the streams trout-y. And I hope, also, that if he accompanies us "campers" through our varied experiences in camp and tramp, he will sometime follow our example and our trail and get great good thereby.

—My companions on these excursions were as follows:—

To "Jock's Lake," H. H. Thompson, then of the United States Treasury, now in the Treasurer's office of the N. Y. & E. R. R. Co.; Mr. Johnson, merchant, of Washington, D. C.; Professor Loomis, then of Manlius Academy, Manlius, N. Y.; and E. J. Benson, merchant, then of Syracuse, now of Binghamton, N. Y.

To "The St. Regis and Saranacs," D. H. Bruce, one of the editors of the Syracuse *Daily Journal*.

To "The Beaver River Waters," Hon. W. J. Wallace, U. S. District Judge of the Northern District of New York; D. H. Bruce of the Syracuse *Daily Journal*; and C. H. Lyman, of the Syracuse *Daily Standard*, all of Syracuse, N. Y.

On the trip, "Booneville to Saratoga," my son Edwin F. Northrup, then eleven years of age.

To "Cranberry Lake and the Oswegatchie Waters," Reuben Wood, the "Captain;" Hon. George N. Kennedy, lawyer and Ex-Senator; Hon. Irving G. Vann, lawyer and late Mayor of Syracuse; John J. Meldram, then Sheriff of Onondaga County; and William B. Kirk, Jr., all of Syracuse, N. Y.; and E. B. White, Justice of the Peace, of Hermon, N. Y.

On the excursion, "Grayling Fishing in Michigan," Hon. S. M. Cutcheon, U. S. District Attorney, of Detroit, Mich.

A. J. N.

SYRACUSE, N. Y., March 24, 1880.

CONTENTS.

JOCK'S LAKE.

                                                                                  PAGE.

CHAPTER I.—Benson discourses of the woods—The start—On the way—Utica—Early morning—Old clothes—Who we were—Breakfast, pipes, coffee-pots, art, and music—Wilkinson's—The "smudge"—Punky!—Tar-oil—A cheerful "good night."..... 11

CHAPTER II.—My first trout—Rain and roads—Walk and talk—Things seen and unseen—Our cabin—Boats and neighbors—A busy camp—Supper—A snug fit—"The smudge! The smudge!"............ 26

CHAPTER III.—Morning in the forest—Camp scene—A trout breakfast — Trout-fishing — Lemonade and "sticks"—Sunset—Heart of the forest............. 40

CHAPTER IV.—Thompson goes a-fishing—Lunch and slumber—Rabbit-stew—"The fly"—Forest sounds—Benson "goes for" a deer—Buck fever—Mimic battles—Benson's story of the deer-hunt........... 52

CHAPTER V.—Sunday in the woods — Veneer—The moral "Isothermal"—Sunday rowing—Evening on the water.. 67

CHAPTER VI. — Jerking venison — Short supplies—Traps—Good night! and farewell!—Out!.......... 72

THE ST. REGIS AND SARANACS.

CHAPTER VII.—On the way to Meacham Lake—Valley of the St. Lawrence—Mountains—Wilderness romances — The Dunes — Darkness — Stumps and dumps—Fuller's................................. 79

CHAPTER VIII.—Meacham Lake—Fuller's—Guides and guests—Programme—Fishing—"Last May"—Up the inlet—Naughty guides—An honest tale..... 86

CHAPTER IX.—Down the outlet—Still-water—A flooded camp—Up the rapids—A damp Editor—Chris.'s jokes—A shot at a deer—"It's mighty queer"—Hunting a trail in the dark—A roof and a dry bed...... 93

CHAPTER X.—The Editor departs—"Vocal chords"—The schoolma'ams—Shaving the Sheriff........... 103

CHAPTER XI.—A new departure—McCollum's—Telegraph poles—St. Regis Lake—Paul Smith's—Evening at Paul's—Jolly guide—The old Professor—Trout from Osgood Pond—Matters and things at Paul's.. 109

CHAPTER XII.—An adventure—Saranac excursion—"Sangemo's" — A merry party — Upper Saranac Lake—Cox's—The sun-browned invalid—Time record—Talk and tobacco—College boys—St Regis Mountain — Pictures — Return to Meacham—The young Reverend—McCollum—Gas-light—Pavements—Out!... 116

THE BEAVER RIVER WATERS.

CHAPTER XIII.—The Judge beckons—"Call a jury"—Black River R. R.—Beach's Bridge—Fenton's—"No. 4."—Beaver Lake and River—Off for Smith's Lake—Wardwell's—"When I git time"—A crooked river and a dizzy sun—The wicked fly—Camp at South Branch—Man lost!..................... . 129

CHAPTER XIV. — "Who-o-o!"—Snakes and boots—Slumber—Rabbits—A mystery solved—The lost is found—A martyr—Albany Carry—Cookery—The Editor overwhelmed—Trout—Smith's Lake—"Syracuse Camp"................................... 139

CHAPTER XV.—Morning — Cross-bills—Surroundings—Wandering trout—Slaughtered babies—Bait vs. fly—"Between hay and grass"—Up the inlet—"Cathug!"—John "the talker"—Fishing record—Broken rod—Judicial triumph 145

CHAPTER XVI.—The Editor's revenge—When it rains—Breaking camp—A stormy exit—Bad blood—Outward—Out 152

BOONEVILLE TO SARATOGA.

CHAPTER XVII.–Correspondence—"Engage Brinckerhoof"—A promise kept—John—"Going in"—Our outfit—On the march—Arnold's—"Old Forge"—College boys—Their story—Up the river—"Stickney Camp, of blessed memory"........................ 159

CHAPTER XVIII.—A morning call—John a "good provider"—Baiting the buoys—Fishing—A broken rod and a sad heart—A Sunday on Bald Mountain—What we saw—A bonanza—A palpable hit—Excursions to South Branch and North Branch.......... 171

CHAPTER XIX.—Migratory impulse and Ned's teasing—A delicate matter—Awaiting John's verdict—Farewell to camp—Eastward, Ho!—Onions—Heavy loads over the carry — Seventh Lake — A good camp site—The lad's cup full—Neighbors—Off for Raquette Lake—A word for "John Brown's Tract".. 179

CHAPTER XX.—The carry of evil renown—The lost pipe—Brown's Tract Inlet — Raquette Lake—Our camp at "Wood's Place"—Rest for the weary...... 187

CHAPTER XXI.—South Inlet—The clerk—Hathorn's Camp—Forked Lake—Steam and smoke—Wind and waves—Bass-fishing by moonlight — Camp among the birches—Camp views—Old Alvah Dunning—"U. S. Mail!" — Camp robbed—The professional camp 192

CHAPTER XXII.—Storm at night—Loose tent-peg—"Muling it out"—Folded tent—To Blue Mountain Lake—Rivers and lakes—Holland's—Ned—John .. 201

CHAPTER XXIII.—Farewell to John—Up Blue Mountain, and sights from its top—Descent—Packing—Wakely—Outward by buck-board—North river—Saratoga and a sleeping-car 207

THE OSWEGATCHIE WATERS.

CHAPTER XXIV. — The conspirators—Off for Cranberry Lake — The 'Squire lost — Clarksboro—Iron Works—Captain and Senator go a-fishing in a cockle-shell—Morning ride to the lake—Reach camp—What the dam does............................... 215

CHAPTER XXV.—Captain's morning call—"Up and dressed"—Guides—Food problem—Brandy Brook—The Senator "yanks"—The Mayor's victory......... 223

CHAPTER XXVI.—Grass river—The Reservoir—Joe Bolio—The Sheriff's joke—Floodwood—"No thoroughfare" — "I've been here"—Rat-hole camp— Council — Return — Trout-pool — "In May" — The 'Squire and the "boss trout"—Grass River trip ended. 228

CHAPTER XXVII.—Brandy Brook trout—Down the river—Trouting on Basin Brook—The solitary fisherman—Stimulating a virtue.......................... 238

CHAPTER XXVIII.—Deer hunt—Up the Oswegatchie —Shot at a deer—Sights and sounds—Cage's spring-hole—My "big trout"—Glorious sport—Landed!— "How large?".. 243

CHAPTER XXIX.—Twilight on the river—"The handkerchief"—"Jacking"—A deer shot—Afloat in a gale—Driven ashore—Prospecting—The building of the camp—Night—Back to the home-camp.......... 252

CHAPTER XXX.—The blue herons—Good shot—Junior shoots a deer—Breaking camp—Farewells—The true story of the "boss trout"—The 'Squire lost—About Cranberry Lake....................................... 261

CHAPTER XXXI.—A didactic chapter—R. R. Lines around the Adirondacks—Entrances—General suggestions.. 269

GRAYLING FISHING—NORTHERN MICHIGAN.

CHAPTER XXXII.—Detroit to Grayling—Down the Au Sable—Boats—Polers—"Sweepers"—My first grayling—Camp—Second day—More grayling—A good leap... 279

CHAPTER XXXIII.—"What I know" about grayling and grayling streams—I. Grayling streams—II. Habits of grayling, etc.—Mr. Wiley's record, six days.. 287

CHAPTER XXXIV.—Across, east to west—Petoskey—Boyne—Charlevoix—"Turner's favorite"—Up the Jordan—Webster's—Jeff., the wise poler—"June's the time"—Trout in the Jordan—Charlevoix—Lake Excursion to Island of Mackinaw—The Island—Mackinaw to Detroit by steamer—Sunset—Talk—Storm—Over the gang-plank and homeward.

JOCK'S LAKE.

Camps and Tramps

IN THE

ADIRONDACKS.

CHAPTER I.

"It's settled that you are to go!" said Benson as he removed his pipe from his lips, and blew a mighty gust of smoke, which dimmed the gas-light of his bachelor apartments like a fog.

"Who settled all that, I beg to know?"

"Well, I've settled it. Here you are, as thin as a shad; you would be pale, only you're beginning to turn yellow, like the covers of your confounded law books; your blood hasn't the vitality of skimmed milk; as to eating, why! our landlady makes a silk dress off from your board every three months; and nothing will set you right like a good time in the North Woods. There, now! That's enough to convince any man what he *ought* to do; but since you haven't enough strength left to form a good resolution, I've made one for you."

"Faithful are the wounds of a friend! even if he goes at

you with a tomahawk," replied I; "but you see, my dear old boy, I can't take the medicine you prescribe,—the treatment is too heroic. If I am the dilapidated individual you picture me, with your rather free-hand style of drawing, how am I ever to endure the hardships of a fortnight in the Adirondacks?"

"Yes, but you see—"

"Yes, I think I do see, indeed; first, the mosquitoes, then the thunder-storms, the long hard tramps, the sleeping out of doors on the ground—what you call camping out—and living on your indigestible flap-jacks and salt pork—and not a drug store or a doctor within fifty miles! Do you think I am a fit subject for such barbarities?"

—"but you see," said he, as soon as I gave him opportunity, "you are not to be the miserable effigy of a man that you now are; you'll begin to mend as soon as you begin to pack up your clothes and fishing tackle; a few miles of corduroy roads will fill you with new desires,"—and he smiled furtively behind a fresh smoke cloud;—"the pure breath of the forest, the sturdy tramp, the free life, the—"

"How about the mosquitoes?"

—"the numberless allurements and employments of camp life."—

"And what do you say about the tremendous storms you've told about?"

"—the fascination of trout fishing, the—"

"Do you deny that camping out will give a man rheumatism?"

"—the glories of mountain and lake and river"—

"Stop! stop! my dear fellow, I suppose you mean by all this to tell me I'll enjoy the trip, and so I doubtless shall if I go, and if I should survive all its hardships."

"I mean to say," said Benson, earnestly, "that to a man whose life is chiefly within four brick walls, and whose every breath takes up some part of the street and its filth, whose daily work is such that his body and health are a daily sacrifice to the necessities of sedentary life,—to such a man there is nothing in the whole range of remedial agents to make him so sound and strong and well and in so short a time, like the two or three weeks he can spare for a trip in the woods. And I want you to go with me! I've set my heart on it. There's a good party of us and I'll take care that the hardships shan't hurt you. You'll have to fight your own mosquitoes, and bear the petty annoyances of camp life; but as for a man's dying in the woods of dyspepsia or biliousness for want of a drug store or a doctor,"—and he threw his head back with an explosion of laughter—"that's the very latest objection to the woods I ever heard!"

I felt that I was answered, and uttered not a word in reply, except to say, "Well, so be it,—I'll go!"

Thus it came to pass that I, somewhat below the average in health and strength at the time, and really needing the remedy my friend proposed, without any forethought or planning of my own, was booked for my first excursion to the Northern Wilderness of New York. When a boy, a fowling piece and a rod were my chief delight, and my choicest recreations were in the "wood lots" and along the streams of my father's and adjoining farms; and a gun in my closet at college had given me many a Saturday ramble over the hills. But I had almost forgotten all the experiences of my boyhood in that regard, and had wholly lost the enthusiasm of those sports, while I was entirely ignorant of the special delights of forest camp life. I therefore anticipated my vacation trip to the woods and the hunting and fishing with no special pleasure, content that it should give me fresh air and vigor.

Many an evening during the interval between the conversation already detailed and the anticipated day of our departure for the woods, Bonson regaled me, in his bachelor quarters, with tales of his adventures on former excursions, and instructed me in forest lore and wood-craft, as, with boyish delight, he drew forth his stores of fishing tackle, his gun and amunition, woodsman's attire and the manifold "little conveniences" an old camper accumulates. His tenderest touch and tones were when he opened his magical fly-book, and fondled the flies that he loved. They were his pets and had been his companions, by many a lake and stream, and associated in his mind with the pleasantest days of his life. Even a half emptied bottle of "tar-oil" evoked an expression of his delight, as he uncorked it and insisted that I should snuff its odors. "You don't like it?" said he in response to my shudder of disgust,—"but you'll see the day when its smell will be sweeter than roses." I did not quite comprehend the remark or the facts it rested upon for its significance.

I had but little care or labor for my own preparation, fishing tackle *et cetera* being thrust upon me by the old woodsman, who, like all enthusiasts of his kind, was already over-supplied, and who bought every new thing useful, useless and ornamental that caught his fancy in the stores where fishermen are furnished. An old, worn-out woolen suit, designed in my benevolent moods for some poor but honest man of my dimensions, and a pair of strong boots, with the avails of a moderate check, were all I was obliged to think about for myself.

It was somewhere among the midnight hours of July 19th that Benson gave the orders,—"All ready! Shoulder pack! Forward, March!" There was nothing to be gained by demurring or pleading that the human spinal column was not adapted to the ponderous load I was directed to take up. So, wriggling into the straps of the pack-basket as best I could, in imitation of the ludicrous contortions of my captain, and seizing a handful of rods and various articles that refused to be packed, I followed him down the stairways of our boarding house; and we bravely wended our way through the silent streets to the near-at-hand rail-road depot. Night watchmen looked warily and suspiciously at us, but the fish rod is ever a passport—except on forbidden streams—and the tramp had not yet developed into a recognized constituent of the advanced civilized community. We escaped arrest and the confiscation of our luggage, and were soon on board our train and hurrying through the darkness to the Utica that refuses to be "pent up."

Arriving at that point, we hastened to bed for the fractional night remaining, leaving orders with the sleepy and taciturn hotel clerk to be aroused at all hazzards at the first indications of morning. The other members of our party had already arrived and were snugly ensconced for the night.

It is surprising how early a July morning can dawn. The edge of the night crumbles away so noiselessly and permits the first gray streaks to steal in so gently and unawares, that he whose custom is to hurriedly rise and prepare for an eight o'clock breakfast, is fain to believe that the break of day comes with the opening of his eyelids. But if good fortune or necessity compels him to witness for himself the phenomenon of an emerging day, he learns to his dismay that a very long and beautiful part of that day has been accustomed to diffuse its glories over the earth long before he has shaken off the thraldom of death-like sleep.

On this particular morning the sleepy clerk passed the word to a faithful porter who battered our doors until we were thoroughly aroused, although in our room it was yet quite dark.

"Here! Now, what *are* you doing?" shouted Benson, as I sleepily and clumsily essayed to put on the clothing I had laid off on retiring. "That won't do,—out with the old clothes! We dress here for the woods, and white shirts and the toggery of the town go into a bag and stay here until we are back to the city again." I protested that we were yet among civilized people, and I should be greatly annoyed to be seen on the streets with the shabby attire I had deemed good enough for the woods.

"Be kind enough to look at your watch, my honest, civilized friend, and then make a note of it that in an hour we shall be out of this place for good;" and as he spoke, Benson tumbled his bundle of old clothes and boots out upon the floor and began his hunt for the gray woolen shirt he had brought for me. Looking at my watch I found it was not quite half-past four o'clock, and even two hours later I knew no stray acquaintance of mine would be likely to stroll down the street.

I had forgotten how disheartening an abandoned suit of old, worn out, dusty, creased and shrunken clothes can be, until I surveyed myself and saw how wholly unpresentable I had become. My personality seemed changed. I was not entirely certain that I was honest. I didn't know but the next moment I should break out in profanity. As for the serene self-respect of an American citizen who had helped elect a member of Congress, I had next to none of it; for did I not bear all semblance to a moderately abased beggar? and did not my very appearance consign me to social oblivion? and would any respectable church in the land permit me to sit in its pews?

However, it was early in the morning, I was in the privacy which the early riser in the city enjoys, and I was wholly reassured by the nondescript appearance of the rest of the party to whom I was speedily presented. Besides, as a psychological fact, I observed that my individuality gradually reasserted itself, and in an hour I was quite as honest, as careful of my morals, and just as much a gentleman, despite appearances, as if I had worn linen and broadcloth and had not been surmounted by a shocking bad felt hat that sloped every way like a wigwam.

Calling the roll, there was Ed. Benson, an old woodsman, and myself, a neophyte, from the same city; Loomis, the Professor, from a neighboring academy, a lusty man of learning, a very Kit North for fish and frolic; Johnson, a hardware merchant from Washington, a good smoker and story-teller, who had won renown and ducats, sailing the seas, and now sought the forest for the first time; and Thompson, our chief, of the Treasury Department at Washington, a bachelor who loved the woods better than most men love their children. Horace, one of our guides, was already in the office of the hotel, a little wiry fellow, silent, shy and tatterdemalion, but destined to blossom and unfold as we approached the familiar woods and streams, and to prove himself indeed "guide, philosopher and friend."

Two strong wagons were speedily loaded with ourselves and luggage, and we drove off in the gray morning in high glee over the hills Northward. If the "Sage of Deerfield," in uneasy morning slumbers, fancied he heard "the rebel yell," so soon after destined to play the dickens with many a soldier lad's dreams of home, doubtless it was the matutinal patriotism breaking out in song and shout of those wagon loads of early travellers in old clothes, as yet unfed and therefore unmindful of the strict code of decorousness and gentlemanly quietude. But he would have forgiven us,—for he too is a loyal lover of the woods and streams.

A few miles out of town, at the foot of a hill among the trees, in a wild sequestered spot we stopped at a little rustic inn, and breakfasted. The ham and eggs and piles of white bread and bowls of creamy-hued coffee disappeared amid the crackle of wit and boisterous laughter and jest, like prairie grass before the leaping flame. There was immense faith, not misplaced, that gentlemanly and civilized dyspepsia had been slain and left behind and that its avenging ghost had lost our trail. The fun had actually begun, and not the least element of it was the reckless and childlike way in which we ate and drank what and when and as much as the appetite moved and the opportunity (not always complaisant) permitted.

Lighting pipes and cigars, each according to his fancy, we resumed our journey over sandy roads, up hill and down, next stopping at Prospect, a town on the Utica and Black River Rail-Road. The wise, care-taking men of our party went about making purchases, of which a frying-pan and coffee-pot were not the least important. Indeed, on these two fundamental facts of camp life hang all the joy or sorrow of the culinary department of tent and cabin. A dozen big, blood-thirsty hunting knives with spick-and-span new leather belts, the latest improvements in air pillows, the most complicated cork-screw-lancet-nut-pick-gimlet-and-carpenter-shop-jack-knife, in the possession of a party, nay, even a mirror and razor, will not bring happiness to that luckless camp where the frying-pan is not, or where the snub-nosed, blackened coffee-pot sings not its morning, noon and evening hymn of comfort and cheer.

Straying into the one humble hotel of the town I explored its domain. In the bar-room were pictures on the wall—faithful representations of battles of the Revolution, the Rebellion and the next war,—masses of men stabbing and "jabbing" each other with bayonets, falling over from the unpictured fire of invisible guns, and posing in death as naturally as if they received on the spot the services of the most accomplished undertaker with ice-chest, embalming process and chaplets of victory kept in stock for battle subjects. There were also horse pictures—race-horses, with legs thrust forth before and behind at angles suggesting the circus gymnast, leaving the brave steed suspended in mid air like Mahomet's coffin, but performing, by suggestion, prodigies of motion which made one ache to wager something on the result of the race,—until the wonder grew, the longer one stared, that they didn't all disappear from the picture, amid the hurrahs of the winners of the contest.

The parlor (for so the tin sign on the door declared it to be) contained a melodeon. I sat down to it, tenderly touched the keys and gently pressed the pedals. It was a consumptive, asthmatic affair, and its vocal chords were in a state of chronic inflammation or else of partial paralysis. It responded, however, in no far-gone invalid tones, and, reassured, I proceeded to question the possibilities of the thing—extorting patriotic sounds more terrible than an army with breech-loaders, light-fantastic-toe sounds which would have made "the Devil on two sticks" dance, (whether with dismay, or with delight that a new temptation had been given to man, how can I say?) sounds that refused to be classified, (such were the possibilities of the instrument, to say naught of the player,)—all to the great delectation of several village lads and one of our drivers who asserted that "he could sit all day and listen to that music!"—a statement I should have implicitly believed had he added—"if my pay goes on all the same." Loomis also, dear kind soul! who had listened through a crack of the door, thereafter seemed to regard me as unfit for treason, stratagems and spoils, and had a tender, warm place for me in his heart.

"All aboard!" shouted the chief, and we were speedily on our way. We drove on to Ohio,—a mere bit of a town made up principally of its ambitious name and a post office, the last we were to see for a fortnight. The horses were fed, while we waited an unconscionably long time for "George," our other guide, who had to be sent for in the neighborhood. Our attention was engaged by a very novel cemetery with unique epitaphs,—a little country church which we respectfully explored,—diagnosing the meteorological conditions from certain ominous clouds assembling for a carnival in the west,—letter-writing at the one little country store,—sleeping on the "stoop" amid difficulties contrived and executed by the wakeful members of the party,—various feats of strength and agility,—and several quarts of milk which we drank and called dinner.

George having appeared, we proceeded on our way to Wilkinson's, well in the woods, the "last house" of civilization, thirty-six miles from Utica, arriving at 7 o'clock, twelve hours after breakfast. Here we stopped for the night and to begin our serious work. The little low, frame-house, a sort of exaggerated bird's nest, browned by age and weather, looked picturesque at that hour. It was situated on a gentle bluff in the midst of a small clearing hewn out of the forest right on the banks of West Canada Creek, which there assumes quite the proportions of a river. The tawny-brown water courses down through the gorge of the mountains on either side, plunging, roaring and foaming among the large boulders which line its banks and are scattered thickly along the bed of the stream, and passes off to the south-east on its way to the Mohawk. Unbroken forests crown the rocky hearted mountains and press down to the water's edge. The darkening, evening-hued sky mingled with the forest green, and the rushing waters sounded their evening anthem amid the stillness of the secluded place.

But what, in the midst of this grandeur and beauty, at this poetical hour, meant that smoke on the grassy plot in front of the house, where the eight or ten Wilkinsons, great and small, from the aged grandfather down to the dirty, toddling baby, were assembled? I ventured to ask Benson as much. "That? why, that's a *smudge*—the greatest institution of the woods!" And he gave me a pitying look for my ignorance, and laughed much more heartily than I thought the subject demanded.

We gladly leaped to the ground from the seats which we had faithfully held down for thirty-six miles, over the last nine of which the road was hilly and rocky. The warm, murky air environed us, languor subdued us, and we were content to throw ourselves down upon the grass. Forthwith a hazy cloud gathered around my head, I experienced burning sensations on my hands, wrists, face and neck. My ears seemed aflame. Was I sick? Had "prickly heat" attacked me? Did I need a doctor? I endeavored to solve the mystery of the haze. I looked earnestly at my hands, and discovered winged atoms of noiseless flight, countless in numbers—dull sparks with wings, that settled quietly down upon me by the hundred and then *burned*. I had not been told of the phenomenon, and it was a revelation. Burn! burn! burn! How they burned! I was almost frantic. I appealed to Benson again; "What is this,—this—these confounded things that I can't see but which bite so horribly?"

"Punky! my boy,—the no-see-ems—the 'cutest little wretches in their line that this country up here produces. They don't sound any horn when they go to business. Oh, you'll get used to 'em. They're not bad. Tar-oil will fix 'em all right. And there's where the beauty of the smudge comes in."

"But I can't endure it," said I, slapping my face, rubbing my ears and hopping about in a transport of nervous irritability.

"Well, you just rush into that smudge, and the punkies will leave you fast enough."

So I rushed. The fierce little gnats left me. The low smouldering fire in the kettle sent up clouds of half fragrant and pungent smoke, which seemed for an instant as luxurious as the first balmy breath of spring. But the next moment I was nearly suffocated and strangling. I rushed out. The punkies returned in stinging clouds, searching every nook and crevice and seam in my clothing and swarming about my head. Back to the smudge I went,—then out,—then in,—the horrors alternating. At length, utterly overcome in the contest, I murmured to my friend, as he slapped and rubbed himself and shared the smudge with me, "Benson, I've come a great ways to be very miserable! Must a man up here murder himself to save his life?"

The humor had pretty nearly gone out of him, but he showed his white teeth in an effort at a laugh, and replied, "There's one hope left,—tar-oil! Let's go for it." And away he went to the pile of luggage near by and hunted up a big black bottle. From this he poured out into his hand a brownish, greasy liquid and rubbed it vigorously over his face and hands, on his neck and well up into the roots of his hair, doing which he gave forth odors which in town would have brought down upon him the censures of the board of health as a nuisance.

"Try it!" said he.

"Can't,—it smells so infernally."

"You'll like it, when you get used to it. Children cry for it, up here."

The stings were driving me mad. I seized the big bottle, and followed his example. Two sighs escaped me,—one at the sickening smell,—one of great relief as the cloud of winged sparks fell back from me in disgust, and I stood once more a free man, but as greasy and brown as an Italian beggar. The battle was ended. I learned afterwards to tolerate tar-oil, then to like its odor, and now I always keep a bottle of it among my fishing traps at home, uncorking it now and then, when the snows are heavy on the earth, to remind me of the summer camp-fire in the wilderness! There is no disputing educated tastes!

Seven of us slept that night in the loft, in feather beds, the rain pouring down upon the roof just above our heads. Wilkinson, as he took the household candle down stairs, bestowed his cheerful good-night,—"Boys, if the punkies get very bad, 'fore morning, call me and I'll bring up a smudge!" But we slept.

CHAPTER II.

The rain came down in torrents all night, to the very best of its midsummer ability under the specially favoring influences of a forest and mountain region. Boisterous West Canada Creek was swollen to a mad river. We sat and conversed under the wood shed, all the forenoon; and while the rain still poured we smoked our pipes, told fishing and hunting stories, whittled, and took our turns around the smudge kettle.

At noon the rain dwindled to a drizzle, and I, the neophyte of the party, born and reared in a land of minnows, bullheads, dace and suckers, went up a little stream near by, and with an extemporized rod and baited hook caught my first brook-trout! It flashed upon my recollection, (or might appropriately have done so) at the instant of my first "strike," that there were several quick things,—lightning, for instance,—the kick of an ugly cow at a milk pail,—the descending blow of a school-teacher's ferule upon the juvenile palm,—the young skater's first somersault,—the bashful boy's blush when the pretty girl of the school smiles on him, and all that sort of thing,—but this trout was a little ahead of them all. In an instant I had him fast upon the barbed hook. The little spirit of activity at the end of the line fairly effervesced; the small pool boiled like a teapot, for there was a tempest in it of one frightened, crazy trout. Three times came the flash, the thrill and the exultation, and three little trout I proudly bore to my companions under the wood-shed; and lightly did I heed the laughter and derisive comments which my fingerlings excited,—for, in the flush of my new experience I was in a state to see visions and dream dreams. In many an experience since that hour, by 'forest stream and pool, I have seen the full vision and realized the dream, then infantile and wingless, but never again did the felicity quite repeat itself of catching my *first* trout.

We had designed,—that is, the Captain had designed for us,—to go up West Canada Creek to "Stillwater," fifteen or twenty miles further, the entire distance to be travelled on foot with packs on our backs, through a trackless forest. The heavy rain had made the travelling exceedingly difficult, and raised and roiled the water sufficiently to destroy all hope of taking fish in the streams for days to come. The council of war around the smudge decided to change the plan of the campaign, and advance, with Wilkinson's baggage and supply train of one wagon, to Jock's Lake (Transparent Lake, on the maps), nine and a quarter miles distant and northerly.

A town road had been cut out, years before, under the delusion that at some time or other this region would be occupied by settlers and the forest tamed. But nature never designed the mountains and rocks and scanty soil for farms. She bolted and barred and locked up these sacred precincts against the plow and reaper,—and threw away the key. The forest of the Adirondacks blesses its worshipers who come with reverent love to its wooded shrines and placid lakes and changeful streams, and sends them forth again rich in the good gifts it holds in store for the forest-loving in heart. But a blasting curse has rested upon every profane attempt to hew down the temples and erect in their stead the granary. The law—not of New York but of Nature—has set apart this wilderness irrevocably to purposes which find little recognition in the marts of trade and the necessities of a teeming population struggling for subsistence.

So that this road had, by disuse, pretty much grown over again, and was now little better, they told us, than "a comfortable squirrel track." We found afterwards that the squirrel who had travelled that track must have possessed a very sound constitution.

After a dinner of bread and milk we set forth,—we five and our two guides walking in light-weight costume, and Wilkinson bringing up the rear with his wagon and two cat-like horses. They had nobly spent their lives in trying to civilize this region and in doing so had learned to clamber over boulders like a goat and to climb a sharp acclivity like a hod-carrier up a ladder. I didn't observe that they had claws, but how they otherwise could so well climb and descend and cling, I could not well conceive. The uneducated horse would have been utterly helpless in their place.

"Is n't this glorious, boys!" said Thompson, as we left the little clearing and, after walking a little way up the river bank along a cow-path, plunged into the forest.

"Glorious!" responded a chorus of four voices.

"That very wet rain has at least cleared the air, and

made these woods smell as fresh and sweet as a baby," chimed in Johnson, whose thoughts doubtless took a backward leap, at the moment, to a certain home circle in Washington.

"And as bright as a maiden's eye", sang out bachelor Benson, with a broad grin.

"Oh! oh!—Why can't you fellows just enjoy this thing in a good, old-fashioned way, without any such far-fetched comparisons, and cheap sentiment!—I say, fellows,"—and Thompson's incipient wrath oozed away perceptibly,—"I say, what tremendous great trees these are! The little chaps have a hard time of it down under these big maples and hemlocks and spruces."

"That broad-spreading beech tree would have delighted Virgil himself, and these, I believe, are the veritable aisles of the dim woods, that Hemans sang," added the Professor.

"The woods are dim enough, to be sure," broke in Thompson, "but they'll be dimmer before we get to camp if you fellows stop to stare at every big tree you see."

So on we trudged with joke or shout or in silence, as the mood took us and the path permitted. Our way was a simple track through a dense wilderness, over mountains, down steep declivities, clambering over monstrous boulders, through slough-holes, and crossing swollen streams on fallen trees,—a bridge sometimes hard to find and always difficult to cross.

The few small birds that inhabit the wilderness flitted about in the shades; a great gray owl right over our heads, disturbed in his dreams, lifted himself from his lofty perch and winged his silent way into recesses of the forest where human foot never trod; the nervous little chipmunk watched the singular invaders of his domain, chippered, and plunged into his hole; a partridge or two whirred and darted off out of sight, almost too swift for the vision to follow; and an occasional rabbit hopped nimbly out of the path and disappeared in the bushes.

This was about all the life of the woods that was revealed to our eyes. But there were tracks in the soft earth by the streams where the timid deer had stealthily crept and fed; scratchings on tree-trunks where bruin had stood up and, cat-like, dug his claws into the wood and stretched himself; and we knew that the helmeted sentinels around us, if they could but speak our language, would tell us of the lithe panther, the prowling and sneaking wolf, and of tragedies among hungry beasts quite as entertaining as histories of man's inhumanity to man.

Wilkinson was compelled to chop out several trees that had fallen across the path, which delayed him somewhat, but the delay was not ungrateful to us. Indeed, as often as the interesting proceeding had to be repeated, we sat down on a convenient and adjacent log with great patience, and superintended the work as wisely as if we were born wood-choppers. Nobody complained of fatigue. If one fell behind, he was examining the geological specimens which the rocks afforded. If he sat down, without a general order to halt, his shoe needed tieing. If one staggered and stumbled, it was only "a confounded root"; pale or flushed,—he was "a little thirsty, you see." Nobody was *tired*, although we trudged and climbed and plunged and floundered and trudged again,—on a bread and milk dinner—for five hours, when at last a gleam of water appeared through the trees, and behold, Jock's Lake!

How often since have I caught that silver gleam of water through the trees, when tramping through the forest! At first there is a little light through the density of the foliage, and on a nearer approach, the glimmer of water;—no shores appearing,—just simply beautiful, clear water shining through the green leaves and the branches. If the sun is bright, the effect is as delightful as any thing seen in the woods.

We emerged from the forest into an opening sloping down to the shore, of perhaps a half acre in extent, where the trees had all been cut away, years before, and the native grass had obtained root-hold and made a very pretty welcome as we threw ourselves down upon the turf bed, thoroughly tired.

A small bark-roofed log hut, built for parties like our own, stood in the center of the clearing, well away from any large trees that in a high wind might take a fancy to fall in our direction. Its dimensions were very modest, the entire structure being but about fourteen feet long and ten or eleven wide, and only high enough near the sides for a tall man to stand upright. One end was devoted to the purposes of a bed room, its limits being designated by a small log running across the cabin, a man's length from the end opposite the door; while the remainder was kitchen, store-room, dining-room and parlor. The bed (soon constructed) was in the true, primitive style of a camper's couch,—hemlock boughs on the ground, "shingled" so that the butts of the boughs were covered by the feathery leaves. These, laid properly and to the depth of four or five inches, constituted a bed which only needed its covering of blankets or rubber cloth to be complete, always "ready made" and quite as welcome after a long day's tramp as the luxurious couch of easy days when sleep comes reluctantly and only lightly touches the eyelids.

"Well, gentlemen," said Thompson, as he drew himself up from a recumbent to a sitting posture, after a brief rest, "I beg leave to suggest to you the eminent propriety of beginning life here on the old-fashioned plan."

"What's that?" struck up three or four voices, with varied degrees of vigor, as the indolent fellows, flat on their backs, kicked their heels into the turf.

"Let's have the plan, Thompson,—no matter what's the fashion," said Benson, as he lazily rolled over towards the first speaker.

"The plan! the plan! Give us the plan!" came out in chorus.

"Why, eating, of course!—I suppose there isn't anything much more old-fashioned than that, except breathing, and that couldn't have had much the start. As for me, I've got my breath all right again, after that rather long walk; and, following the logical order and the natural inclination, after all this exercise, I propose next to eat.—I say, Wilkinson, where are your boats? Some of these crazy fishermen who have been talking trout all the way from Utica, want to now just get out their tackle and try their hands at catching a supper for this party,—and a good one, too;" and by this time Thompson had lifted himself heavily to his feet. "I'm not selfish,—these chaps may have the fun of taking the first trout."

Wilkinson, like a merciful man, had seen to it, first of all, that his beasts were unharnessed and hitched to the hind wheels of his wagon and fed in the wagon box with a bundle of hay and a supply of oats brought with him from his barn; and he now approached.

"Them boats, boys, are hid up in the woods. You ain't never sure of finding a handy thing like a boat, up here, when you want it, if you don't put it out of sight. Folks don't exactly mean to steal, but they'll use 'em and don't always leave 'em just where they got 'em. My neighbors"—

"Neighbors!—where on earth do your neighbors come from, Wilkinson?"

"Why, they're all around—that is,—I mean they're all one side of me, that's a fact!—and the nighest of 'em is well on to seven miles from me;—and he ain't much of a neighbor, to be sure, for he lives all alone, and he's one of your darn mean, half-squatter, half-trapper and whole-lazy fellows that ain't one thing nor another. Then beyond him, three miles further on, there's some more, and they're likely folks, too,—got families and work for a livin'. I tell you a man's got to work some for a livin' and help somebody else to live,—a wife and a chick or two, may-be half a dozen of 'em, of his own,—to be a first-class neighbor, up here. And my impression is—it mayn't be worth much—that a man that don't work any and don't try to make livin' a little easier for somebody else, runs a mighty big chance of not makin' much of a neighbor of himself anywhere."

"But I don't see, Mr. Wilkinson," interrupted the Professor, who seemed amusedly interested in the disquisition of the backwoodsman,—"I don't quite see that you have fairly established your original proposition that you have neighbors, when the nearest person is seven miles away and no neighbor at all in any proper sense of the term."

"Oh, very well," replied he, doubtless stumbled by the assumed gravity of the Professor. "You mean by neighbor the man in the next yard, I suppose, that knows what you had for breakfast in the mornin', and who you brought home to dinner with you, and hears your wife when she spanks the baby, and—"

"Never mind him," said Benson, "he's a pedagogue, and takes everything like the multiplication table. He don't realize how the imagination of a genuine backwoodsman sweeps around for twenty miles and takes in all the people of a circuit as his neighbors."

"But the boats, Wilkinson, where are they hid? I'm as empty as a last year's chipping-bird's nest, and I must have some supper!"—and Thompson emphasized his remark by patting his stomach, in a patronizing way, with his open palms.

"You can't find 'em—they're over beyond the spring, up the hill a little ways, behind a log and covered up with leaves. I'll go and show you, and help you get 'em down to the lake;" and as he led the way two or three of us followed.

The boats were drawn from their hiding place down to the water and launched, and found to be in good condition and reasonably tight after their rest in the woods. Benson and the Professor, the ardent fishermen of our company, already equipped, stepped aboard, shoved from shore, and proceeded to a point indicated by Wilkinson as likely to respond to their skill.

Meanwhile, our camp was assuming a busy appearance. The luggage had been unladen from the wagon; an open fire, out of doors, had been built for cooking purposes; and the smouldering fire of chips and leaves, making the inevitable smudge, had been duly inaugurated—destined to be our pillar of cloud by day and of fire by night. Horace, the silent, had found a modest and civil tongue, and with nimble fingers was dissecting the baggage and preparing for our simple forest housekeeping, bestowing the supplies in the cabin, and shaking out the blankets, and in fact, doing almost everything, while at the same time watching the coffee-pot hung over the fire. George, the big, strong, noisy, good-natured fellow, could swing an oar like a walking beam all day, and compel the proudest forest king to cast his crown to the earth after a few moments of his vigorous assaults with the axe; but about camp he was pretty nearly good for nothing.

Horace, on this occasion, sent him into the nearest timber to chop wood for the night, and this he did so faithfully, that in a short time he had a large pile of heavy sticks ready for the all-night fire.

"Here we are—and here's supper fit for a king!" sang out Benson, as that worthy approached, holding up a string of trout. The ponderous Professor, following hard after, added—"and, gentlemen, if there's to be a division of labor in this camp, please allot to me the task of providing brain food for this company, as found embodied in the speckled trout of Jock's Lake."

It was almost no time before the trout, with a little fat pork, were in the frying pan; and Horace watched them as they hissed and sizzled and curled, and turned them at the opportune moment, and at length pronounced them done.

"And I must confess, well done, thou good and faithful cook!" said Thompson, who seized a little trout by the tail and swung it deftly to his mouth and closed his teeth upon the delicious morsel.

"I enter a protest," exclaimed the lawyer of the party, "against any unequal distribution of the assets of this firm; —share and share alike is a part of the original contract between us. Besides, a clerk in the United States Treasury ought to have learned to treat the public property that comes within his reach a little more sacredly."

"If you were on ship-board, Thomp.," said the sailor-merchant, "you'd be rolled on a barrel for that trick."

"It strikes me, gentlemen," retorted Thompson, "that by your common consent I am your Captain. Therefore, I make the laws. I here and now"—and he munched his trout with a hungry man's vigor—"ordain and establish—is that good law phrase, Mr. Indignant Lawyer?—that while we are in camp, and there's plenty to eat, every man shall eat when he's hungry and drink when he's dry, and to his fullest capacity—so far as is consistent with the safety of his buttons, which every man must sew on for himself."

"Agreed! agreed!" on all hands; and the speck of war vanished as Horace announced supper ready at the rude table in and along one side of the hut.

In due time the hearty meal was finished, and twilight deepened into darkness. We gathered before the fire, or clung affectionately around the smudge, lighted our pipes, and chatted and told stories until the early bed-time hour.

Then eight tired men laid themselves down, side by side, across one end of the single apartment, upon the bed of fragrant boughs.

"It's a snug fit, boys!" said the bulky Professor, "and if dignity is to have any privileges, in this party, I should like an inch or two more room."

"We're all on a common level, here," responded the Captain, "—just now, at any rate; but if you talk of privileges, I'm the official personage that wants 'em."

"I say, Benson," whispered the Neophyte, "how the dickens do you fix your boots to make a comfortable pillow? Mine don't fit my head; the heel of one of them seems to be sticking into my bump of philoprogenitiveness."

"Well, you *are* a new camper, I should say!" said Benson, as he examined the rude head rest; "you've got the coat in the wrong place—under your boots, instead of on top. There, now!" as he folded the coat and arranged it, "your boots are meant for foundation and your coat for superstructure. To-morrow I'll get out the flour sacks, down in the depths of my pack basket, somewhere, and fix you up the jolliest pillow you ever slept on,—hemlock and spruce twigs,—that'll make you dream of Araby and spicy breezes, and all that."

"Horace!" shouted the captain, "now shy your hat at the candle over there on the cracker box, and put out the light! It's high time this party was asleep. The sun gets up here about as soon as the early bird that has always been held up to me as an example."

"All right! Shy away, Horace! I'm fixed"—"and I" —"and I"—"and I."

The old hat performed its mission, and eight men all facing one way, closed their eyes and importuned balmy sleep.

Instead, came the soft sing-sing of the hominivorous mosquito—with sense so keen that in the midnight-hour of the darkest night he goes straight to the best feeding ground on the nose of his victim;—as a honey laden bee flies homeward to his nest in the hollow tree;—as the bolt from a Remington or Sharp's rifle cleaves the air for a thousand yards and strikes the bulls-eye;—as a creditor unerringly follows, with his little bill, the young man of vain hope who neatly turns a corner, dodges into a club-room, hurries to catch a street car, and when caught at last wipes dust from his eyes as if a great and recent family bereavement had overtaken him and weighed him down with grief which should not be disturbed by sordid cares—and duns.

So came the mosquito,—the *avant courier* followed by a host like Xerxes's army—that is, perhaps—how could one tell, in the dark! The single note swelled to an orchestral performance. Slap! slap!

"By Jingo!"

"Ugh!"

"Horace! George ! Up with you!—you careless fellows," sang out the Captain; " you forgot the smudge!"

" For Heaven's sake! the smudge!" groaned the Neophyte.

"The smudge! the smudge! or we die!" fairly yelled the Professor.

And eight men sat bolt upright in the darkness, thoroughly wakened by this terror of the night—the gentle-winged, sharp-tongued mosquito.

At last,—the smudge aiding—our senses succumbed, and eight men slept.

CHAPTER III.

Morning always comes—to the gay reveller who has exhausted all the night in feasting, drink and song, and drunken laughter,—to the weary watcher by sick beds,—to the fever-tossed, the sorrow-laden, the care-burdened,—to the toilers and guardians of the night,—to the dwellers in palaces, pillowed on down,—and to men in a hut, sleeping on bushes, all in a row. It didn't skip us,—and eight men yawningly hailed the early dawn, and crawled out of the cabin.

The sun was just peering over the mountain across the lake, and flinging his silvery-golden beams down upon the sparkling waters. The forests in their morning freshness wore a tenderer green. The sweet morning air was fragrant with balsam and spruce and mossy earth. The cross-bills flitted in startled and darting flight from our cabin roof, to the neighboring trees, and back again, uttering their quick, sharp notes, in search of the crumbs from our table. Nature's own morning hour, unvexed by the smoke and dust and busy rumble and roar of civilized life, had come to the wilderness.

"How do you like it?" said Benson, after quietly watching me a few moments as I gazed in evident, keen enjoyment of the scene. "'Beautiful' isn't any word for it,—

is it? There's a good deal more than that word conveys in such a morning and such a scene as this. Oh, I remember"— and the eyes of my good friend, who usually concealed the really earnest and noble side of his nature under a veil of humor, were dreamy and his voice low and musical as he spoke, "—I remember the first summer morning I saw in the wilderness, a dozen years ago. It came like a revelation of what—yes,—of what heaven might be, if it should be brought down to the earth. I suppose every man has a little poetry hid away in him, somewhere. That morning was the key that unlocked mine. The forest seemed a vast temple,—the worshipers all reverently silent; and the sun for the first time, as it slowly rose and seemed to gaze benignantly on lake and forest, became Father of the day and not its King.—Ah, my boy," after a moment's silence, "that seems a good while ago, though, and I've had some hard knocks in the world's rough and tumble since then,— but this sunrise sends me all the way back, over the years, to just such a scene as this and to just such a delight as you now experience in seeing a forest sun rise for the first time."

"Well!" called out the Captain, who was already busy about camp, *fussing*, as Johnson styled his work,— "Well! if it takes you fellows much longer to determine whether that's the break-o'day or not, you won't very soon have break-o'fast!" at which desperate attempt at a joke nobody smiled but himself. "We've got to have some trout for breakfast," continued he, "and I shall order out another detail, if Benson and the Professor don't proceed at once."

I accompanied the fishermen to the lake shore, towel in hand, to make my morning toilet. After speedily accomplishing this, I half sat and half reclined on a rock, and watched them as they rowed out to the fishing-grounds,— their voices and the dipping of the oars gradually growing less and less distinct as the boat noiselessly glided away. Behind me, at the camp, busy preparations were being made, as I could see. The smoke rose from the fire, thin and pale, in the bright sunlight; Horace was moving hither and thither with spoon and dish and pail, while George was seated on a log humbly peeling potatoes,—that being the least skilled labor of the forest kitchen; Thompson had a thousand little things to do, but at this moment was suspending a pocket mirror by a nail driven into a log of the cabin, out of doors; Johnson was examining and cleaning his rifle; Wilkinson was feeding and watering his horses and preparing for his return homeward after breakfast;—while the circling forest looked silently on. The whole scene was so new and strange to me that I forgot that I was a member of this body politic and had the duties of a citizen to perform with the rest. However, as I was the youngest, and the Neophyte at that, and was not counted as knowing the things "worth knowing" in the woods, my inactivity attracted no attention. It was my fortune, indeed, to be treated throughout the trip as a guest and admitted to all the good things and spared all but the inevitable labors. Thanks to the dear old boys!

The fishermen soon returned with all the trout required for the morning meal, and shortly after we were seated at our humble table on the long stout pole which was supported by crotches. Even the Professor was not heavy enough to break that down, although he had a distracting way of smashing nearly every thing he sat upon.

"Now, boys! I call this a model breakfast," said Thompson, after five minutes of steady eating that forbade speech; "—even if I did supervise its construction."

"You don't mean to claim the credit of this,—do you, Thomp.?" half indignantly queried Johnson. "Horace is the pilot that brought this breakfast safe to harbor,—you were nothing but a land-lubber passenger."

"Gentlemen," said the Professor, "Horatius is the genius to whom we are indebted for this concatenation of delicious edibles. It was he who, by the wave of his spoon, evoked cosmos from chaos,—who"—after a mouthful, he went on—" who transmuted things to be weighed and measured and put into bags and bundles and boxes by the grocer"—another mouthful—"into"—

"You'd better beach your craft," broke in Johnson, "for I take it you've got into deep and troubled water and are overloaded with your 'concatenation' and your 'cosmos' and 'transmuted.' Horace can't stand it to have you abuse him in this way. I think, myself, there were never such trout as these, nor boiled potatoes whiter and mealier, nor flap-jacks so big and light, nor maple syrup richer, nor coffee that went straighter to the spot,—but I don't quite like to have you lug in your 'cosmos' and 'chaos' here."

"Oh, let him go on," said Benson;—" he's comparatively harmless, so far. The last trip I made with him he was full of 'nectar' and 'ambrosia' and the 'feasts of the gods.' We're lucky if we get off with 'cosmos' this time."

But despite the talk and banter the eating went on, until the hearty breakfast was ended, and Horace ceased from his labors at the frying-pan, and George, the waiter, gladly heard from one and another, "No more!"

After breakfast Wilkinson returned home with his horses, but leaving his wagon until he should come for us; and as he disappeared in the forest, the Neophyte, experiencing for a moment a sensation of home-longing, thought: "So the curtain drops between us and the outer world, to be raised some days hence, revealing—no one knows what!" He never felt precisely that way again, but never failed, in similar circumstances, to feel for an instant a certain sense of loneliness and helplessness.

Now began, in earnest, the real life that we had come to enjoy,—life in a primitive fashion, far from the cares and distractions as well as the luxuries of civilization, cut off from all men but our own chosen company; the life of the savage, with all the bad elements left out, unconstrained but not lawless, jovial and free but self-respectful, natural but certainly not barbarous; a too short period of alternate work and rest, of sport in fishing, rowing, shooting, swimming and in doing a thousand little things, important on such occasions to be done, but difficult to report, and perhaps of interest only to the actors themselves.

"Wilkinson is a good enough fellow," said Benson,

"but I never feel quite as if I was in the woods, for good, and my camp life had actually begun, until I and my party are left alone.—Well, now boys! who's going a-fishing? Don't all speak at once, for it's one of the cardinal virtues, in the woods, not to catch any more trout than can be used. Lot's of sport and no waste."

"Not I, to-day," said Thompson; "this camp isn't quite in ship-shape yet, and I propose to get it into first-rate living order before I try the fishing. But, mind! when I do start in, you fellows might as well unjoint your rods,—I shall put you all to everlasting shame and confusion!"

"Oh, the modesty of the man!" exclaimed the Professor; Benson adding, aside,—"but he isn't so very wide of the mark, though. That's always his way in camp,—fussing, and fussing, fixing up all the little conveniences, until everything is in apple-pie order, and then he starts into the fishing with a will."

It resulted in our all going out upon the lake but Thompson. At the proper point, our two boats were brought to anchor and we began fishing with bait, and very successfully. The trout averaged about half a pound, few of them weighing over three-fourths of a pound. Just as is always likely to happen in bait-fishing, I, the least experienced fisherman of the four, took the largest trout caught that day. I was happy enough, even with bait-fishing, at the time, for I knew of nothing better; and, for the sake of that memory, I do not care to speak disparagingly of the humble angle-worm as a lure. But I must add that, when afterwards I learned with moderate skill to wield the

2

fly-rod, and in a fair fight captured my first trout with the fly, a little blush of shame mantled my cheek at the recollection that I was so happy on that first morning at Jock's Lake. I can imagine many compensations that will come with old age,—if, indeed, it shall come,—for the losses of enjoyment that befall impaired physical faculties; but what shall come in the place of camp and tramp in the Adirondacks, and the glorious joy of casting the fly over the pools and in the rapids of forest streams, and the leap and dash and play of the gamy and beautiful trout!—This, however, is not what I was thinking of, as I sat in the boat that morning and drew in trout after trout, as handsome and as gamy as any I have since seen.

"Hi! Hi! that never will do," exclaimed Benson, as I was about to lift to my lips a cup of water dipped from the pure, spring-fed lake; "you'll be sure to be sick if you drink that. Here,—pour a little of this 'enlivener' into it," bringing out from his pocket a flask of brandy.

"I never drink, you know."

"No matter—I don't drink, myself, except in the woods,—but you must take a drop here, or we'll have an inconveniently sick man on our hands."

The last argument was conclusive, and I poured some of the contents of his flask into the cup of water, and drank. We continued fishing, but I speedily lost interest in the sport. In fact, by the time we reached camp, again, I was pale and weak and sick. The delicate stomach I had brought with me into the woods had rebelled at the unaccustomed stimulant, and gave me fair warning not to repeat the affront.

And I venture to record, right here, that I have since, in various forest excursions, tramped and camped and slept, become wet and cold, hungry and tired almost to desperation, and drank water from all sorts of rivers and lakes,—and my whole stock of liquors on a trip of two or three weeks could be comfortably carried in my vest-pocket; and that the only time I was ever sick in the woods was that morning when I took lake water "mollified" by Benson's brandy.

It is always easy enough, after breakfast, to fill the coffee-pot again, or, better, make tea, with which to quench thirst, if no spring can be found. But it is desirable to have a flask of liquor along,—brandy or whisky,—for emergencies, as medicine. I fear, however, they are not always hygienic considerations that govern the commissary as he includes in his supplies bottled ale, and sundry black bottles of stronger stuff.

Possibly, one ought to have a little regard for the welfare of the guides of the wilderness,—brave, faithful, hearty and generous in the main, but some of whom, through the example and well-meant importunities of the parties they accompany, become intemperate and in the end worthless characters. Many of them, however, taking warning from the fate of others of their class, use liquors very sparingly, generally after their hardest work is done, and prefer a cup of tea, hot or cold, to any other stimulant.

Our party, good fellows, temperate and free from all bad

habits, yet believed in the old-fashioned idea that a thoroughly good time in the woods and entire safety from a "change of water" involve a little whisky, together with lemons and sugar.

"Here, now,—that will fix you up all right," said Thompson to me, when we reached camp, directing my attention to a cup on the rude table. "I've concocted a punch in that pail that will make you fishermen happy again. I knew you would all come in heated and thirsty, —and perhaps cross if your luck wasn't good. Fill up, boys! and drink to—ourselves!

"What? Not any? What do you mean?"

"Oh, I think I'll give those lemons another squeeze and try lemonade. I don't believe I was exactly seasoned right for anything stronger;" and upon that I fashioned a drink that cooled and refreshed me, and speedily put me in as good spirits as any of them. And after that, the lemons after being put through the squeezer for the punch-pail were laid aside for my special use,—and nobody felt aggrieved.

A little before sunset, George rowed me up the lake two or three miles, on an exploring expedition. The lake is five or six miles long and about one mile wide, lying like an irregular crescent, curving westward and nestled among the mountains. The shores are, in the main, rocky and firm, but at the outlet, southward, they degenerate, and, not far below, the stream wanders off into a marsh, or pond, nearly overgrown with lily-pads,—a famous resort for deer. The lake itself is fed by springs and has no inlet of any consequence; and its waters are as pure as Nature, in her own chosen laboratories in the forest-clad mountains, can produce. It is the natural home for trout, who relish the best things as well as an epicure or the most cultivated aristocrat,—which the trout family is among fishes.

Every sense was keenly alive to enjoy this unwonted scene, as I sat and half-reclined at my ease in the stern of the boat, while the strong, steady oar-strokes of my guide swept us out from shore upon the smooth bosom of the water. The morning had been beautiful,—the approaching evening was not less so. After his strong and stately course through the sky, the sun, about to depart, seemed to mellow and soften with tenderness toward the green forests and silvery waters, and I easily fancied he lingered reluctant to say good-night to so much loveliness. I am sure that with almost a human touch he kissed, with something very like a "good-night!" the lake, and then the timid foliage that crept down to the eastern shore, and then the sturdy, robust forest trees as they climbed up the mountains, and at last the mountain brows themselves. And was he not looking backward, with a little mist in his eye, for one more glance of recognition from his beloved forest children, as he journeyed on with unabated vigor in his tireless course towards the new morning?

The stillness of the hour was unbroken by converse. There was so much to receive that I hardly had a thought to utter; and my honest guide, accustomed as he was to the beauty and tender awe of such a scene, in the forest life he had led, and ordinarily unobservant of it, was yet touched upon the lips by a hand he could not see, and held his peace.

At length, sweeping around to the west, shortly after the sun had descended below the mountains, I went on shore to get one look at the heart of the forest. My guide sat on a rock at the water's edge by his boat drawn up at his side, while I alone entered the dense and now darkening woods. There was something fearful in the stillness. The solemn silence seemed like the hush before the bursting of a storm, and the ancient trees frowned from their lofty heights,— I half thought they were gathering up their knotted arms to strike down the curious invader of their sacred halls. As I advanced, an undergrowth of small trees, in time to become the successors of the heavy giants above them (so does Nature, in man and tree, work out her eternal law of succession and change),—impeded my progress, and the darkness was still descending.

However,—such was the marvellous fascination of the hour and the place,—I pressed on, calling occasionally to my guide, and awaiting his responsive call, to ensure my being able to find my way back to the boat. But, at length, I discovered that I was walking in beaten paths. Tracks of animals of no mean proportions were behind and before me. All the legends of wolves and bears and panthers that I had ever heard or read, flashed upon my memory,—and with one more call to George, I turned and hastened back to the shore.

I was content with my one glimpse, by twilight, at the forest's great and solemn heart; and having once, alone, and in such an hour, touched it with my own hand and listened to its throb, I have felt the awe of that experience evermore.

We returned to camp, the inevitable smudge, the campfire, the pipe, the story and joke and banter, and, at last to our bed of boughs,—one genuine day of our vacation ended.

CHAPTER IV.

Two days after, Thompson had arranged every[thing about] camp to his satisfaction,—among other things, [had] erected a flag-staff and run up the American flag, w[hich] we thereafter vigorously cheered as we nightly re[turned] from our fishing or our exploring. He had gone o[ut row]ing, near by, or bathing, and amused himself watch[ing the] rabbits that came out at nightfall after they [had become] accustomed to our presence, but had not yet wet a li[ne.]

"Now, gentlemen," said he after breakfast, this m[orning,] "I propose to have a day of fishing. I shall lay a[side my] official responsibilities, and, on your own level, proce[ed to] show you what an old fisherman can do when 'he's [got] good ready,'—and you," turning to me, "shall b[e my] companion."

"That's wise," said Benson,—"to choose one a[s green?] [as you] who never has caught trout before, and wh[o will] therefore be duly impressed with your prowess."

"I am convinced," said the Professor, "that ou[r] Captain has in mind to claim the combined catch [as his] own. There is nothing in the way of impuden[ce that] might not be expected of a man direct from Wash[ington.]"

"Jealousy! pure jealousy! gentlemen. Horace, y[ou are] to go with us," added Thompson, turning to that [worthy] who was busy with his housekeeping duties; "and a good lunch, for we shall be gone all day,—and don't forget the lemons for this cold-water-man's drink."

As we strolled along towards the boat,—Thompson and I,—Thompson said, "I didn't want any of those boys to go with me to-day. They are all fish-mad. They are glorious fellows, but they have been bitten by trout, and nothing satisfies them but killing trout again. Now, I love fishing dearly. There is no sport like it for me. But there is a vast deal in fishing besides catching fish, and that is what I want to get to-day. I want to explore this lake,—to enjoy this scenery a little,—as well as to fish. They wouldn't be willing to do that,—it would be just fish! fish! fish! all day with them, and if a fellow ventured a little sentiment, there'd be no end of banter. But you are new to the woods—no trout has ever bitten you yet, although your day is pretty sure to come if you repeat this kind of a trip a few times,—and I have seen you looking off on the lake and the mountains, in the morning and at sunset, in such a sort of way, that I have judged that you enjoyed these things enough to go a-fishing on my plan. So, I have asked you to go with me."

"Yes," said I, "this is all new and very delightful to me. On this trip I mean to catch the forest if I don't catch many trout. I can't be content to go away with only a dim memory of what, when I stop to look at it and feel it, impresses me more deeply than anything else in nature ever did."

"Agreed, then," replied Thompson, "that for to-day, we shall fish as lazily, and talk as sentimentally, and keep silence, when we choose, as freely as we may happen to desire."

By this time Horace had come down to the shore, where we were standing; and in a few moments we were out on the water, pointing directly for "Old Bald Head," a rocky promontory across the lake, where stood a bark shanty which had sometime been occupied by a fishing party.

We fished a few rods off the point, taking eight splendid trout, and then moved on, up the eastern shore of the lake. We fished at various promising places, went ashore to find cold springs and to gather spruce-gum, and passed nothing of interest without examination.

At the head of the lake, and on the western shore, right on a little bluff, close to the water's edge, we landed to take our noon-day lunch. On a big soil and moss covered rock we spread our blanket for a couch, for we proposed to ourselves the oriental luxury of reclining while we feasted. Two great trees, rooted upon the rock, spread their leafy arms above us, while the heavy forest pressed down behind us and lent additional shade and the delicious coolness of the dense woods. Horace built a smudge in a little hollow near by, on the windward side, and then drew out the big basket of lunch, and made a refreshing lemonade. And "then and there," lying on the softest of couches, looking far down the lake and out on the evergreen forest on the shores and mountains in the distance, we lunched,—stopping between frequent "bites" at excellent sandwiches of ham and soda crackers, or cold trout and johnny-cake, and sips of lemonade, to admire and comment on the wonderful beauty that surrounded us. The smudge graciously sent its tiny clouds just above our heads, and spared our sentiment the mocking tears that come—and end—in smoke.

Then we lighted our cigars,—for this was Thompson's holiday,—reclined on our backs, gazed up where the smoke wreaths were floating among the green leaves, and were silent. Cigars finished, and fanned by the softest breezes stealing over the pure water, we dropped off to sleep,—every one of us in a blissful nap, more delicious than the sweetest, stolen, summer sleep in a country church during a drowsy sermon. Good, kind wolves! most excellent bears! and self-denying panthers!—whose tracks and traces we thought we saw on the forest side of us,— many thanks to you for that peaceful and undisturbed slumber!

The responsibilities of station vex the soul of authority, even in slumber,—and the Captain wakened. Our oriental table and couch had wooed and lulled us for an hour and a half of the noon-day; and we quickly gathered up our basket and blankets, bestowed them and ourselves in the boat, and pushed from shore.

Down the lake we rowed again, chatting of hunter's and fisherman's exploits, of the beauty and exquisite loveliness of the scenes coming upon us gently and "with a sweet surprise" at every turn,—our happy thoughts and reveries, when we ceased talking, keeping time and tune with the sturdy and steady oar-strokes of the wiry and willing guide. We hardly cared to fish, and when we did, the dropping of our hooks in the water was like smiting a mirror into fragments,—so utterly quiet and glassy-calm was the surface,—and the trout, as well as we, seemed to be in a revery after a lunching of their own.

We had been told of a rock on the west shore, "as big as a house," placed or misplaced there by some convulsion of nature. It was visible from afar, and we put ashore near its base. Thompson and Horace sat on a rock by the water in the shade, while I paid a visit of curiosity and respect to the mysterious stranger. A tree had fallen against its side, and on that I climbed as far as the tree went and then clambered on a precarious footing up the nearly perpendicular side to the top. It was over twenty feet high, and about thirty feet by fifteen on the top, and in general outlines rectangular, a conglomerate boulder, with shining quartz intermingled with sand stone. I pecked some of the jewels from his crown and put them in my pocket for souvenirs. The grand old fellow had a history but he was mute and silent in our presence, and refused to be interviewed.

After our early supper, we all gathered about the camp-fire, as usual, to talk over the affairs of the day and to enjoy the pipes and jokes and stories.

The rabbits, by this time, had become quite accustomed to our presence, and came out after sunset from the shrubbery at the upper end of our little farm, to feed. We were greatly ammused and interested in their play, and watched them with the spirit of a naturalist, until some earthy-minded soul suggested that rabbits made an excellent stew.

"Aye! Aye!" said Horace, "I can make a rabbit stew fit for any man in the party."

"Let's have 'em!" hoarsly whispered that insatiate fiend, Benson.

"Yea, it is not *meet* that men should live on fish, alone," gravely declared the Professor—he of the well lined abdomen—"and I opine that"—

"Well, well!" said Thompson, as he half rose from his seat in apparent disgust, "if this scholastic gentleman means to make a pun on flesh and fish in this high-handed manner, I suggest that somebody shoot *him*,—he'd make a stew for half a tribe of cannibals."

"Such wrath in celestial minds?" retorted the Professor; "may not one signify his occasional desire for meat, without danger of being made that which he desires?"

But at this instant the Neophyte, who had quietly taken a gun from the hut, pulled the trigger and ended the wordy controversy and the career of a fat rabbit at the critical juncture. The rest of the rabbit family hopped and skittered off into the woods instantly, and Horace speedily prepared the game for stewing in the morning. When once we had tasted flesh again, all scruples against killing the pretty creatures vanished, and we went to our butcher's as regularly as the family man at home,—always, however, as a matter of safety, ordering a rabbit stew.

In the afternoon, on the following day, Thompson,—who evidently still loved the woods and waters for something besides what he could catch with a hook,—graciously taking me as his companion again, went down the lake to the outlet, where we left our boat and scrambled down over rocks and fallen trees, near the rapid stream, to "the fly" (vlei?)—a broad, shallow, marshy pond, half overgrown with lily-pads—where deer love to feed. We gathered wintergreens on our way, and pitcher-plants by the shore, picked up a feather from an eagle's wing,—that was about all—but heartily enjoyed the sunshine and shade and the weird stillness.

The forest has its sounds, even on the quietest of days,—the slight rustle of the aspen leaves, perhaps,—the low, sad note of the wood bird flitting through the shade,—the startled chirrup of the chipmunk,—the scream of an eagle soaring high above the trees,—the buzzing of flies in the sunshine,—but the total impression is of a stillness almost appalling. But there come days in the woods, and especially nights, when nature becomes restive and wakens from this sleep of her forces. The air so soft and gentle becomes nervously tense and strong as the muscles of a rudely awakened giant. It stretches out its invisible arms and swings and sways them until the wild, rushing sounds roar through the trees; dashes upon the placid waters, and the waves run to and fro as in fear or in madness; sweeps and plunges down through the mountain passes, and the mournful wail of the startled recesses rises in a passionate prayer for peace again; seizes the monarchs of the forest and wrestles and strives with them until they groan in the mad grasp of a power that cannot be grasped again, for it is the intangible power of the air. And then, the storms!—the wild carnival of the lightnings,—the horrid bellow and rattling savagery of the thunder; its roar and crash among the mountains,—and the blinding floods of rain, descending as if the clouds were huge catapults hurling their wild, watery missiles down with all the wrath of war! If the stillness was appalling, so is this, the other possibility of an Adirondack day.

But on this occasion the giants were all asleep, and Thompson and I stepped over and around them unconscious of their presence, and declared there was nothing half so charming as an afternoon ramble and scramble in the Adirondack woods. So do we all, in our daily lives, walk among the unseen elements of tragedies, happy to day in the sun-shine,—to-morrow sitting with bowed heads and aching hearts in the darkened home where the storm has burst, the bolt descended, and there is an untold desolation.

We were in camp again, in the evening. "Boys," said Benson, "Horace and I have a little business on hand. This camp hasn't had a mouthful of venison yet,—and there's plenty of it running around loose in these woods. We're going for it."

"Put him in the hold!" shouted the sailor-merchant,— "he's gone daft! Too much lake water, no doubt, and too little 'enlivener.'—You don't propose to go out of camp this dark night, do you?"

"That's the programme, my dear, innocent friend. You don't suppose I mean to shoot a deer up there where Neophyte shot the rabbit, do you?"

"But it's darker than a cellar,—and it's almost sure to rain."

"So much the better," replied Benson. "You can never 'jack' a deer in a bright night,—and this sultry air makes the flies bite, and a deer's sure to go for the water when the flies pester him as they will to-night.—Hurry up, Horace, with the 'jack'"

Horace had prepared the 'jack-light,' which was simply a piece of bark nailed upright on the semi-circular edge of a bit of board so as to form a rude reflector, within which was placed a short candle, the whole supported by a stick thrust through a hole in the front seat of the boat.

Benson finished loading both barrels of his heavy shot-gun with buck-shot, examined everything to see that there should be no accident in the darkness, or mis-fire at the critical moment. Then the two went down to the landing, and we heard the muffled grating of the boat as they pushed off from the rocks and disappeared from sound and sight down the lake. They were to land at the foot of the lake and then clamber and scramble as best they could, in the darkness, down through the pathless woods to "the fly," where a water-soaked, half-rotten, leaky scow awaited them. In that unreliable craft, at the uncanny hour of midnight, they were to light up the "jack," and "float" for deer. Horace was to paddle as silently as a snake glides over the grass; the "jack" was to throw its light in front, leaving the boat and its occupants in the shade; the hunter was to sit close behind the jack-staff, gun in hand, ready in an instant to shoot at the "two globes of fire" which the eyes of the deer would resemble when staring, confounded at the light, or to shoot at his body if luckily that should be brought into relief.

All this was to be done, it had been explained to me as being the Neophyte,—but at the last the deer itself might fail to perform its part of the drama. There's many a slip, I was told, between a deer and a shot. Sometimes the deer has grown wise through experience, and in its small brain reasons that if a candle explodes and roars and stings the innocent spectator with a stray buck-shot one night, it may do so another night, and is not to be trusted to approach; and the deer betakes it to its legs and shows no globes of fire at all. But an unsophisticated deer is very curious,—and, possibly, would know good and evil,—and upon seeing a bright light, and nothing more, stares and stands, if he hears no noise and does not smell the foe, until the hunter approaches to within fifty, forty, thirty feet. Then there is nothing to do but to keep one's nerves steady, silently raise and aim the gun, and pull the trigger. If, however, the shooter is new to the experience, he is likely to be more nervous than the deer is,—to forget to shoot, sometimes, or to shake as in an ague fit, and to commit indiscribable blunders,—in other words, to have "the buck fever." So that, after all, "jacking deer" is not such a one-sided affair as at first it would seem to be.

Meanwhile, we had withdrawn to the hut, and refilled and lighted our pipes. A quartette of us, seated like so many tailors on the blanket-spread couch, were, with joke and laughter and snatches of song and whistled airs, fighting the mimic battle of "kings" and "queens" and "knaves." Nothing more fearful was done in these battles than that "clubs" smashed "hearts," the vulgar "spade" won victories over the aristocratic "diamond," and the mathematically impossible came to "pass,"—one counted more than ten, and to this magic quality even royalty and knavery succumbed. The Neophyte,—an inveterate keeper of a diary,—by the same tallow-dip, with a cracker box for a table, was writing up his notes for the day, and gathering up the little odds and ends that, woven together, make up the warp and woof of forest life in camp.

But the longest and jolliest evening in the woods, as well as out, at last brings bed-time, be the couch that of luxury or the bed of boughs.

Some hours after, I half awoke, and by the dim light of a flickering and sleepy candle saw Benson, all wet and dripping, with slouched hat and long rubber overcoat shining with moisture, holding his gun in his hands, and standing just within the door; and by his side stood Horace with a deer flung across his shoulders, the legs drawn around his neck like a huge, fantastic necktie. In an instant every one of us was wide-awake, and while the rain was beating in torrents upon the rude bark-roof of our hut, Benson, while removing his coat and boots and concocting a reviving punch, began his story:

"Well, boys, we've got him—sure! But what a time we've had! You see, it was as dark as ten pockets boiled down into one when we got to the foot of the lake. You couldn't see a thing. We thought we wouldn't light up, for there was no telling but we might scare every deer in the neighborhood. So we floundered along, keeping near the stream, guided by the sound of the water and the little let-up of the darkness where the trees were separated and the sky had a chance to look down.

"By good luck, we found the old scow where we left it when we hunted it up the other day. We found the old tin can under the seat and bailed out the water, but the wretched craft leaked like a riddle, and we had to do a little more plugging up of cracks and holes before we dared to start off with her."

"How on earth did you do all that, in the dark?" asked Johnson, "and without anything to caulk her with?"

"Oh, Horace lighted up the jack, and kept the light from flaring by holding his coat all around it,—made a regular dark lantern of it, you see. And I,—well, I parted with a good piece of my shirt-flap for caulking purposes. A man in the woods can't be particular about these little matters.

"Well, finally we rigged the jack in the boat and got afloat. Luckily it didn't rain just yet, although the air was as full of moisture as a balloon is of gas. We went down the 'fly' forty rods, perhaps, about where I thought, the other day, a deer ought to come in, if anywhere. Before we got very near, I touched a match to the candle and the thing sputtered a minute and then went out. A drop of water had got on it, somehow. I thought we were in a fix, but after two or three matches had been held to the wick, the water dried off, and the blaze started. Then I saw what a glorious night it was for jacking. The darkness was so thick that you could cut it. That I could see by the candle-light. I thought some of slicing off a few nice pieces to cover Horace up with;—but it wasn't necessary,—a deer couldn't have seen either of us if he had worn spectacles.

"Horace paddled as if he was creeping up to a camp of Comanches,—slowly, and so still that at one time I almost looked around to see if the fellow hadn't given me the slip, and gone ashore again. I had enough on hand, though, looking out under the jack in the space covered by the light to see the first show of deer, and listening with both ears and my mouth to hear a step or a splash. A little rascal of a frog startled me, once, jumping off a lily-pad into the water. 'Gracious!' thinks I, 'there's a deer that's got scent of us before I've got sight of him,—and he's off in a minute, if that's the style of step he's taking!' But that was a false alarm, of course, and one that Horace wasn't fooled by, either. Then I had the dickens' own time with the punkies and mosquitoes. Something like five million of 'em settled down on me and kept off five million more that wanted to get on but couldn't find room. I didn't dare put on any tar-oil. Might as well've staid in camp as to have advertised in that way,—a deer would've smelled me a quarter of a mile off. And I couldn't slap 'em, for a deer is keen to hear the slightest sound, and he can tell a frog-jump from a slap at a mosquito as quick as he can wink. So, all I could do was to rub my hands together, as well as I could and hold my gun,—and get mad enough to stand it."

"But tell us about the deer, old fellow, and not be bothering about the frogs and mosquitoes," interrupted Thompson, who grudged the loquacious huntsman the time he took, at that hour of the night, to relate all the marvels of his deer-hunt.

"I begin to doubt," said Johnson, "that you shot that deer at all,—you make so much of—"

"—the accessories," added the Professor, by way of helping out.

"By Jove," continued Johnson, "I believe you just cast anchor, down there, lit your pipe, and this deer crawled into your boat to be sociable, like,—and then you bloody pirates cut his throat."

Benson, who by this time had relighted his pipe, smiled triumphantly and continued—"I can show you the buckshot holes in his skin, to answer that,—and there's the back of my hand, and here's the blood-spots on my neck to satisfy any gentleman that the five million were down there.

"Well, (puff, puff,) as I was going on to say, we paddled along as carefully as if we were right in the midst of a whole herd of deer fast asleep, and were as afraid as death of 'em, for fully twenty minutes, when I heard another little splash in the water and something dripping. Horace heard it, too,—and it wasn't any frog-jump, this time,— and he just turned that boat, bow on, towards that sound, as if the old scow was on a greased pivot no bigger than a pin,—shoved her ahead four or five rods, and there stood my deer! He's a good looking buck now, although somewhat in a heap,—isn't he? But you should have seen him then! He was up to his knees in the water, feeding on the lily-pads; but the moment the light caught his eye he straightened up, and stood like a picture,—head up, nose a little thrust out as if asking questions about this new thing. May-be he thought it was some new sort of fire-fly that made a great flourish,—possibly, he imagined there'd been a new style of moon invented for specially dark nights and that this was the way it generally rose,—perhaps, however, he was just dazed and didn't imagine much of anything.— At all events, just the minute I thought I was near enough to put a sure shot in, I shook the boat, just a trifle, and Horace stopped paddling;—I sighted along old "Sure Death" and blazed away.

"My! what a splashing and dashing there was! As bad luck would have it, the gun kicked like fury, when I pulled it off, and somehow the jack was knocked over and the light put out. Where the candle went to, I don't know.— Horace had another piece in his pocket, and we lighted that, and then went hunting for our deer. I knew it was ours, fast enough, by the kind of racket he made in the water. He had managed to get ashore, but we tracked him four or five rods and found him, and Horace cut his throat. Then we dragged him into the boat, came back to the landing, and started through the woods. Just then it began to rain. We were fairly walled up in the darkness, and the rain just poured. We managed to keep our candle burning about a quarter of the time, and the other three quarters we were plunging into holes, over rocks and bogs, in the dark; and Horace was 'most as dead as the deer, while I carried the gun and the jack, and was the worst done-for man you ever saw. But I got my buck!—and there he is! and if you fellows are not grateful for the venison he'll make,—you go, next time. My story's done."

"For all such blessings may we be duly thankful!" sonorously responded the Professor.

CHAPTER V.

The morning came, and with it a day of alternate thunder and storm and sunshine,—and our first Sunday in the forest. There were no fine clothes in camp; no church-bell sounded across the water; the big, family bible and the religious weekly had not journeyed thither in Wilkinson's wagon; but somehow all these had left some sort of impress on men with sprouted beards, worn and torn attire, —men who had changed their skies but not their minds.

"Gentlemen," said Thompson, as we emerged from the hut after breakfast and strolled down to the rocks on the shore, "I'm not very straight-laced, and don't pass, at home, for a Puritan, by any means; but I never fish in the woods, on Sunday, unless I am desperately hungry. I'd make a sorry show as your spiritual teacher, I suspect, although being your Captain, I have the right to make the proper Sunday laws of the woods for you. But, boys, if you want to fish to-day, my advice is,—don't!"

"It is not difficult, worthy Captain, to accept your advice," said the Professor, "in the presence of these reverent forests and yonder pure and placid lake, with the sky above us as benignant here as where it bends over our Sabbath-keeping homes."

"That's put rather sentimentally, isn't it, Professor?" inquired Benson; "but if you get right down to hard-pan, and say that a man's a man, no matter what sort of clothes he happens to have on or who's watching him, or where he happens to be, I just agree with you. And if he is only a veneered man at home, the veneer'll come off up here and he'll be whatever he is,—may-be a heathen."

"You can paint and rig an old ship that's worm-eaten and rotten," added the old sailor, "and it looks about as well as a bran'-new craft with every plank and timber in her as sound as a bell; but the long, lonely voyage tells on her, and the storm don't care for the paint,—she's pretty sure to go to wreck. That's the way I suspect it is with your 'veneered' men."

"The man who yields obedience to law,"—and the Neophyte took a hand in the discourse,—"simply because of its sanctions and penalties, or because it is respectable to be law-abiding, is not law-abiding at all,—he's simply law fearing or dishonor-fearing. He's the sort of man that breaks down suddenly and to the astonishment of every body, when he moves to a new country, loses the influence of old and restraining associations, and simply becomes his natural self. Your genuine man obeys law—moral as well as civil, civil as well as moral—because it is right to do so. Indeed, I don't think a man makes a very good Christian who joins the church to keep out of hell,—takes out a spiritual fire-insurance policy and calls it being religious on principle. It isn't,—it's being religious on policy."

"But do not you lawyers find that it is the lower motive,

after all, that mainly influences men to obey civil laws?" asked the Professor; "and do you imagine, for a moment, that laws would be generally obeyed if the punishments of their infraction were removed?"

"That is for the philosopher and not the lawyer to answer," replied the Neophyte. "However, it is apparent to any one but a dull observer, that criminal laws and their penalties really influence only the smaller portion of civilized mankind; but the line of demarcation, properly drawn, would be as great a curiosity as an isothermal line across the continent. Station, rank, wealth or poverty, education or ignorance, in themselves do not fix the line,—it sweeps high, it sweeps low, it runs strangely, to human eyes,—but it runs by a law as clear to the Mind which can see the man that is hid in the body, as the isothermal line is to the wise student of nature. It goes by character,—and character isn't reputation or position."

The pipes were all empty. The breakfast dishes having been cleared up, and affairs at camp tidied up in general, the guides sauntered down to the rocks where we sat.

"Well, what next?" said the Captain. "From my small text about not going a-fishing, you men of words have spun a rather lengthy sermon,—enough for to-day, I guess."

"I propose," said Benson, "that we take a row around the lake. It's better than sitting here—the Professor may break loose next. To avoid all criticism, I'll suggest that the guides do all the rowing, and that we reduce the number of oar-strokes from a hundred and fifty to—say—

thirty a minute. That will be about a comfortable church-going jog."

"Better leave your rod at camp," said the Captain—"your Sunday morning resolutions would fade out dreadfully quick if you saw a trout leap, while you were on your 'church-going jog,' if your rod was in the boat."

And so it was ordered and done. The two boats, bearing our entire party, swept out upon the lake, followed the winding shores, rounded the points and penetrated the bays, in a leisurely way, while we enjoyed to the full the freshness of the morning and all the beauty of the varied scenes.

A thunderstorm in all its majesty and fury burst upon forest and lake. Forewarned by the distant but fast approaching roar and the marshalling of great banks of clouds in the sky, we pushed ashore, drew our boats out of water and up under the trees and speedily constructed a refuge by turning them bottom side up with one end resting on the low limb of a tree. Like a true Adirondack thunderstorm, it deluged everything around us for a few moments, and then hastened on with unabated fury, out of sight and sound. The sun shone brightly again, and we speedily resumed our quiet journeying.

Our Sunday dinner was a triumph even over Horace's former exploits, for. in addition to everything else, we had the most delicious bits of Benson's buck.

The evening hour approached, and by tacit and common consent we all strolled down to the water's edge, stepped into the boats and pushed out a little distance and anchored, while the guides remained at camp and completed the homely duties there.

It was the most peaceful scene and hour we had yet enjoyed. Even the midges and mosquitoes, which always preferred to remain on shore and never pursued us twenty yards from land, had fallen away from us like summer friends.

Our talk was of times gone by, of friends absent, of topics hardly suggested by our surroundings; while the gently descending darkness and the balmy air and perfect serenity of nature attuned our thoughts to higher themes than we ventured to dwell upon in the rough-and-tumble of our daily camp life in the garish light of day or even at the nightly camp-fire.

So passed our Sunday in the woods,—not wholly without its good influences.

CHAPTER VI.

Monday morning awoke fresh and brisk, like a town rousing from a holiday rest. Every man of us felt that he was beginning genuine forest-life anew.

"Boys, I tell you it pays, even up here in the woods," said Benson, as he stepped out into the bright morning light, "to have Sunday come once a week. Something has turned back the clock or the almanac with me, for I feel a year younger than I did Saturday night."

"And I," said the Professor, "feel it in all my nature—and especially in my wrists and finger-tips—that I must again ply my rod. My piscatorial appetite is strong again. I must catch and kill—or I perish!"

"It takes people different ways, I see," said Johnson, "but I always did feel that after I had been in harbor awhile I wanted to up with the anchor again and put out to sea."

"Well," added the Captain, "why don't you go along, the whole of you, and fish to your heart's content?—only, I give you fair warning, this venison is to be jerked, and we're about out of provisions, and you can't have the boys with you.—Here, Horace, fix up the racks and you jerk the venison; and George, you'll have to foot it out to Wilkinson's and pack in some flour and sugar and some other things that Horace will tell you about. You can go out to-day, and come back to-morrow."

The morning's fishing was very successful,—the trout themselves having apparently shared in the general Monday morning enthusiasm, and almost gleefully responding to the fisherman's call. On the whole, Monday was a triumph.

On the following day George returned, and gaunt famine —in the form of short supplies—departed by the shortest trail to some less fortunate camp. A single letter had found its way to us, and that, so far as news of the outer world went, was read aloud to the whole party.

There was rifle-shooting at a target, this day; and the *palma* was awarded to "the Lemonader," with great good nature, and a tribute to the nerve-steadying effects of the victor's chosen beverage.

The Neophyte had, for days, wearied his brain with plans for capturing some of the rabbit family alive. He longed for the cheering and humanizing influences of a menagerie. The care of a dumb beast, he thought, would exert a liberalizing influence on the entire party of fish-slayers. This day he devoted his finest talents to the construction of two "figure 4" traps, with which he was wont in boyhood to entrap the confiding wood-chuck,—alas! sometimes, to his discomfiture, capturing (a Greek present) the odor-bearing skunk. In this contest with rabbit wit and cunning, he signally failed. The cracker-box was too small, the tub, ditto,—and hairs, not hares, were the net result. Besides, chipmunks,—villainous little thieves!—were the allies of the rabbits, and sprung the traps. But at last a little chap ran into our hut, and him we caught and confined in a bark-cage then and there made.

So did we beguile the hours of the afternoon and evening.

So did not, however, Horace; for he hovered around the rack where the sliced deer-meat was slowly drying and smoking over the fire he had built under it, and, after curing it to a turn, stored it away to be carried out of the woods as a wonderful product of woodsman's skill, to be shown and nibbled and pronounced delicious—after it was explained that it was "jerked" venison.

The days went on, and we found renewed pleasures in the old employments and sports. There were the rowing, the fishing, the bathing, the rifle-shooting, always, and we invented new diversions and enjoyments almost daily,— small and unimportant to speak of, but wonderfully important to be done and enjoyed. We had our terrific thunderstorms, depositing floods of water, rather too frequently, but they were always so grand, that if we got a wetting there was no grumbling,—it spoiled no clothing and broke no business engagement. The fishing was all that our more ardent fishermen desired; and there was something for every taste and fancy and desire. Even the screams of the owls by night—and those other sounds, as of human agony that once we heard,—brought something to us..

At last, there came an evening—our last in our woodland home—when we rowed out on the beautiful lake to say our final Good Night! to all its loveliness. It was more beautiful, if possible, than ever before. We had come to know and love its features like those of a dear friend. We had seen its face in all moods and phases of feeling. To-night it was placid,—quiet and sad, we thought,—or was that a reflection of our own emotions? As the evening shades crept steadily and heavily down from the mountains, and then the full-orbed moon arose and dispelled them again, and we lingered, reluctant to say the parting word to the lovely water with the home-spun name,—we, hovering between two worlds, the depth above and the depth below,—and looked abroad on forest and mountain and lake, in their supernatural glory of light and shade, and felt—as who does not when bidding farewell?—that we might never behold them again, who shall blame us if, for that moment, we idealized all this charm and beauty and mystery, and gave it a human soul,—and if we stood on the shore, at last, and waved a silent adieu with emotions like those a lover feels as he bids the maid he loves a long farewell!

Many a time, that evening scene in its surpassing serenity and loveliness has come to the heart of the Neophyte, in his slumbers by night,—but his waking vision has never since looked upon the beautiful water, to which he that night silently said "Good Night, forever!"

The noisy morning came, the bright, strong, sensible sun, and the preparations for our departure, which consumed nearly all the forenooon. It was surprising how much packing we had to do, considering what an impudently small load we had when the packing was done. We had, in fact, pretty much eaten up the burden we brought in. Wilkinson's phenomenal horses were on hand, with their owner, and by noon we were ready to move forth.

Horace and the Neophyte led the van, and plunged into the forest. The long, weary tramp to Wilkinson's was begun. The vanguard were fortunate enough to see that beautiful sight—a deer by day-light. When his vision was blessed by this sight, the Neophyte felt that his cup had run over. The timid creature gazed—we gazed—but a step forward, and she sprang from the water's edge and disappeared in the forest.

For four hours, through mud and over rocks and streams and mountains, and through thunderstorms, we steadily tramped,—every step elastic and strong, and without fatigue, (such was the triumph of Nature's Medicine!) until, safe and sound, we all reached Wilkinson's again.

At three o'clock the next morning we were up and away to Prospect, twenty-one miles distant, where we caught a railroad train, and at 10½ A. M. were again in Utica. There we were restored to cleanliness, our good clothes, hotel cookery, time tables; and, with these restored, we separated, going our several ways, and our delightful, long-to-be-remembered expedition "to Jock's Lake" was done.

The Northern Wilderness,

OR

THE ST. REGIS AND SARANACS.

CHAPTER VII.

One July afternoon in 187—, and subsequent to the events of the last chapter, the Editor and I, after a long journey by rail, found ourselves at the Ferguson House in the thriving town of Malone, Franklin County, N. Y. Our faces were turned towards the Northern Wilderness.

Passing many gateways to the land of promise, we sought this as an entrance to a region of peculiar delights, and one remarkably full of benefits to the tired seeker of a vacation. We were to climb up, southerly, out of the Valley of the St. Lawrence, into mountains and forests where the lakes were cold, the air invigorating and bracing even in the period of summer heat,—the spruces and balsams taking kindly to both the latitude and the altitude.

Twenty-five miles to the south and well into the woods, lay Meacham Lake, where a comfortable forest hostelry was maintained by A. R. Fuller. This was our first objective point.

In an hour we had dined, our livery was at the door, our luggage packed, and with two gentlemen from New York, of like destination, we were in our seats, and away with a dash.

We were granted a perfect day, a good span of horses, an easy-riding wagon, an intelligent driver, and for many miles a good road; while our chance companions proved to be most agreeable. For the first third of the distance our way lay through an ordinary, cultivated, farming region; then we began to climb the foot-hills and at length the mountains, in a rougher and more rocky and less cultivated region, until at length, in the density of the forest, we lost all reckoning.

The first mountain that we ascended, in the open country, gave to our view the broad, vast valley of the St. Lawrence, in panorama. We climbed and straggled up on foot, halting and turning as often to catch the changing scenes as to rest from our weary labors. Far off to the north, north-west and north-east extended below us the plain, in field and woodland and town, the shining belt of the distant river faintly gleaming under the July sun; and the receding Canadian hills, in the remote distance, at length mingled their hazy blue with the tenderer azure of the sky. The higher we climbed, the grander the scene and the wider the scope of vision, although the barrier of hazy blue far off continually lifted its front, a shore to the sea of sunshine in the valley below.

There was a strange thing. Here and there, in the valley-plain, arose, bold and rugged, like a vast boulder, a mountain with almost perpendicular sides that were bare and looked to be rock,—detached palisades, or, lost and forsaken antediluvian monarchs with their rugged forest crowns yet on their heads. Or, were they massive towers of Babel, built in some mad freak by the old Sons of the North, or, fortresses of defense against Odin and Thor? Whatever they were, they are now striking features of scenery to one climbing toilsomely up the mountains to the forest. And if you journey thither, pray you may have a bright July day over your heads, with a sea of sunshine rolling its gently swelling tides from the foot of the mountains you climb to the far off blue-haze mountains behind which the Canadian wilds stretch away to the Arctic Sea.

There are many romances connected with the wilderness; —of hermits who sought the depths of the forests to hide some sorrow or crime from the gaze of men;—of refugees from foreign lands, nobles and princes at home, who came hither to bury themselves in utter obscurity until a new political revolution should restore them to favor and fortune. Even a Bonaparte came to the solitudes, with wealth and pomp, and left a story that will be repeated as long as men love the marvellous.

"Old John Brown," for years, lived in the wilderness as the friend and counselor of the colored settlers to whom Gerrit Smith, with good will but poor wisdom, gave lands for farms and homes, and "his body lies a-mouldering in the ground," at North Elba, where he had lived, while his soul has been marching on in the events of well nigh a quarter of a century since he died on the scaffold.

Then come the homely and pitiful romances of gigantic business enterprises in the wilderness, gone to wreck and ruin. This strange region is a vast bed of iron-ore. Untold wealth is hidden in the mountains. Strong men have grappled with the problem of its removal; money and thought and skill and tremendous toil have been expended lavishly, to that end; but all to no purpose. The wrecks are scattered here and there, monuments of ill-directed energy, and warnings against any future endeavor of the kind without the use of such modern appliances as shall absolutely conquer the stern resistance of this region to all attacks upon its treasures.

In our journeying, before we reached the dense forest, we touched upon the edge and saw the desolate home of one of these latter romances, in the town of Duane. And it will do to be briefly historical, perhaps,—since in that consists the principal part of the romance.

There lived in the city of New York during the Revolution, and long after, James Duane,—a lawyer and statesman, useful, influential and famous in his day, and honored by President Washington with an appointment as the first United States Judge of the District of New York. He performed the rare act, as he became old, of voluntarily laying off the robes of office. Upon his resignation, he removed to Schenectady, and there died in February, 1797, leaving one son and four daughters. His grandson, James Duane, having acquired, by marriage with a daughter of William Constable, a large tract of territory in the then named town of Malone, (from which the town of Duane was afterwards formed,) removed thither from Schenectady with his family in 1825, and made his home nearly ten miles from his nearest neighbor, the most remote settler in the forest in all that region. He and others entered upon the project of iron manufacturing in 1828, built the necessary works, formed a settlement in due time, spent a fortune, and disastrously ended the experiment in 1849.

We passed through the ruins of this enterprise; and our driver told the story of the Duanes, as we rode along between the miles of maples they planted by the road-side and the miles of stone fence they built. He pointed out the spot where the old mansion stood,—burned mysteriously soon after the elder Duane died,—and we saw for ourselves the deserted barns scattered through the meadows along the river bottoms, the weather-beaten, abandoned houses of the laborers and other subordinates, and the various signs of the life and activity that must once have prevailed there. And we saw a man of slouched figure, in butternut suit, slovenly and heavily bearded, carrying a scythe on his arm towards the poor, barren meadow,—and he was a Duane! This poor remnant of the great house of Judge Duane bowed gloomily to us as we passed and gazed curiously at him, and we left him behind.

But the scene was far different—so the story went (and it was afterwards corroborated by others)—when the first Duane came. He was dashing, rich, gay, aristocratic, high-blooded, and he came like a prince. His progress to his forest estates was a triumphal procession. His house rivalled in luxury the manor of his ancestors, the Livingstons. The work of hewing down the forest went on bravely under many hands, and the wooded hills resounded with shout and axe-strokes and the rumble of toil.

Then came the troops of friends and associates from the east, brave men and fair women, for summer and autumn sport. There was feasting and revelry. There was wine and frolic. There was stag-hunting with hound and horn and caparisoned steed. There was, indeed, in this rude American forest, the luxury, gayety, roystering and wild sport of baronial castle and estate in the old world in the old days.

The driver told us all this in his homely way, as he drove on, and said—"and that rough fellow you saw back there is the last of the Duanes in this neighborhood."

The twenty-five miles were dreadfully drawn out, and long before we reached our journey's end the double darkness of the dense woods and the night settled down upon us. The conversation waned, and we were most busily employed in watching our way, as well as we could, up and down the hills in the forest, wondering what was ten yards ahead of us, and exercising our faith in the sharpsightedness, sagacity and true-footedness of our steeds, and in the experience and watchfulness of our driver. At one time, as we were plunging in the darkness down a hill, there was a shake and a shock as of a railroad collision, and everything came instantly to a stand-still. Our driver shot out of the wagon over a front wheel as if propelled by a cannon, while we, wedged in by the seats and the luggage, found ourselves most unceremoniously huddled, in a most miscellaneous way, in the bottom of the wagon. A reconnoissance discovered to us that no serious damage was done, although the driver complained of a bruised shoulder, upon which he had very suddenly alighted. Nothing but a small, stubborn stump projecting into the road was the occasion of this uncomfortable commotion, but it was enough to make us all doubly strain our eyes the remainder of the journey in watching for further offending stumps.

We were glad and tired, when, at ten o'clock, we drew up at a little log-house, all in darkness, on a lake shore, and the driver shouted in cheerful accents, "Here we are!" We were just in time, too, for in a few minutes the rain poured down upon the roof in torrents, and the night took on an inkier blackness. Our host, Fuller, speedily provided supper for his hungry guests, and without much ado we climbed up stairs and into our comfortable beds.

CHAPTER VIII.

The morning came, bright and fresh, and presented us in excellent condition and spirits. We found that we had descended upon a delightful wilderness home, upon the northern shore of Meacham Lake,—a body of water stretching one and a half miles southward, and one and a half miles in width, surrounded on every side by primeval forests, and on nearly every side by mountains. The little log-hotel in which we had slept and eaten faced toward the water, and across its front ran a rude, ample verandah; while behind it was a small clearing where the household vegetables struggled, under inhospitable conditions, to meet the modest expectations of their cultivator, and where, under the yearning gaze of Fuller's excessively steady span of horses and a very mild cow, a small field of diminutive oats was ripening and the thin ghost of a hay crop was maturing.

On the east, a few feet distant, was the older log-house, which once served as the only dwelling, and where under former auspices and administrations there had been wild times of sport and carousal. It was now simply the "guide-house," and also contained Fuller's little shop where a rod or a gun could be repaired as neatly as skill and a fine set of implements could do it. It was also the general meeting place of the sportsmen and male tourists. On the racks and nails and pegs were hung guns, rods, fish-baskets, landing-nets, powder-flasks, shot-pouches and rubber boots and coats,—indeed, about everything one could think of as ever going into the woods; while up stairs was the one large sleeping apartment of the guides.

On the other side of the "hotel" was a new frame-dwelling, "for gentlemen accompanied by ladies," in accordance with a law of civilization which always has the approbation of the fortunate monopolists, but which inevitably strikes the uncomfortable excluded as an invidious distinction not consistent with the broad application of the principle underlying female suffrage.

The Editor and I, belonging for the time to the excluded, were only able to say that the building looked like a comfortable sort of barracks, and we endeavored to persuade ourselves that our own snug quarters under the sharp-pitched roof of the log-house must be more comfortable and cozy than anything found in the more modern and pretentious structure.

A rambling and well ventilated log-barn and stable in the rear, a log pen for the hungry and restless deer-hounds, and a wood-pile commensurate in size with the length of the winters and the depth of the snow in this region,—both of which Fuller was accustomed to meet, endure and face down, all alone, with his personal pluck and presence,—completed the picture.

As it happened, for a few days we four were the only guests occupying the log house, while two or three families from New York and Brooklyn, including nurses and several children just graduated from their cradles, were occupying the more modern building. The gentlemen had waxed rich, but had not ceased to delight in the experiences of forest, lake and river. A young fellow of the party, in the flush of his first trouting season in the wilderness, contributed his robust enthusiasm and full flow of ruddy spirits to our enjoyment.

At the guide-house were several men, hired by Fuller for the season to act as guides and boatmen for his guests when required; while here, also, was "Jimmy," the Irish lad of all work, an indescribably funny fellow and as full of genuine Irish wit and humor as an egg is of meat.

So much we saw and learned as we stretched our legs along the grassy slope in front of the houses, lounged under the breezy pines, and explored our surroundings, in the morning hours.

Taking boats and guides we went to the south end of the lake, where the stream from Osgood Pond enters, looks down the lake, and, turning hastily to the west, departs again with hardly an effort at forming an acquaintance with the beautiful lake to which it has contributed,—the stream becoming at its exit the east branch of the St. Regis River, and in due time emptying into the St. Lawrence. We descended this outlet to the head of the rapids, walked around them to a bridge on the road leading from Fuller's to Paul Smith's on St. Regis Lake, and there wet our lines and tried our luck for the first. A pleasant forenoon was thus passed, and we returned to the house for dinner.

In the afternoon, we again went to the inlet and to the

outlet, both of which we fished faithfully, but with indifferent success. We had, however, made the acquaintance of a pretty lake, and a charming bit of rapids below the bridge, and were content.

That evening, as we were assembled in the "guide-house," we discussed plans for future exploits and expeditions. Even in the easy-going, half-indolent vacation mood one feels the need of a programme. We construct a plan of operations, seat ourselves in it, as in a boat, have faith, and lazily wait for strong arms to row us along. It is a comfort to feel that we have proceeded in a business-like way, even in our recreation; and our conscience commends us much as when we have taken out a life-insurance policy, and so, like a good citizen, have done the proper thing for our family.

On this occasion, we consulted our worthy host and the brown and shaggy oracles about us, for information as to the best fishing resorts and how to reach them.

"There's the inlet and the outlet," said Fuller, "and the rapids below the bridge."

"But we tried them faithfully to-day," interrupted the Editor, "and, I must confess, with some disappointment."

"Well, last May bushels of trout were taken there," was the answer.

"It isn't May now," retorted the Editor, "and I imagine the trout are off on their summer vacation."

It was just dawning upon our comprehension that the landlord of a forest hotel, however clever a fellow, was not likely to voluntarily recommend fishing resorts much beyond the sound of his dinner-horn; so I interjected the query, "How is fishing down at Paul Smith's?"

"Oh, well," answered Fuller, doubtless anticipating the next question would relate to modes of conveyance, "you don't need to go there for trout. Osgood Pond, this side of Paul's, is better than anything he can show you, and you can make a day's journey there from here and get all the trout you want. Start early in the morning, boat it up the inlet, take your baskets full of trout, and come back."

And we went to bed on that programme.

The next morning we were up bright and early, and bustled around as if there was a twelve o'clock edition of an afternoon paper to get out, or an important lawsuit to be called at the opening of court. But, for reasons not then quite apparent to us, nobody else hurried; our landlord was easy and quiet; our guides found a world of important affairs to attend to before starting; and the morning was well advanced before we four and our boatmen were off and away to Osgood Pond.

Our little flotilla moved gaily down the lake. The strong-armed oarsmen, with well-seasoned backs, swept the wavelets with even strokes, and the sensation of delicious comfort and ease we experienced, as we were borne along without effort over the liquid surface, was something to remember. The Castle of Indolence has nothing to equal it in its entirely respectable and righteous laziness.

At the inlet—the river from Osgood Pond—we entered upon a sluggish, winding, alder-fringed stream, which, for utter silence, weird loneliness and an interest all its own,

could not be surpassed. Somebody suggested fishing,—
and nobody objecting, four rods were jointed and rigged,
and four leaders with their delicate flies were launched
forth.

Then on we went, and on, with logs here and there disputing our passage, until dinner time, when we landed at "Hog's Back," near McCollum's clearing, where a little cool stream comes into the main river. We built a fire, roasted the trout we had taken, opened our baskets and feasted in a rudimentary way with the woodsman's keen appetite and zest. Again we proceeded on our way up-stream, the crookedness and the snags and logs increasing every moment. It was all so strange and primitively wild that the difficulties of our progress were scarcely observed but to be enjoyed, and we were unconscious that the day was declining and that it was impossible for us to reach Osgood Pond before night-fall. Our most excellent hypocrites, the hotel guides, knew that before we started, but we had been left in blissful ignorance.

A thunderstorm broke upon us. We drew our boats up on the shore and sought the shelter of the trees. At first they protected us admirably, but after a time the leaks in the leafy roofs became uncomfortably numerous. Starting a "smudge," we made ourselves as jolly as possible, and speedily the storm, after the fashion in the Adirondacks, passed along.

And now we discovered, upon consulting our guides and our watches, the ignominious fact that Osgood Pond was out of the question. When we came to know good and

evil, there was suppressed wrath in our hearts. We [
victims,—we had been duped,—we were long-eared [
mals. But we had enough sense left to order a ret[
and returned to the house as rapidly as possible—our gu[
displaying a mastery of the art of rowing, on our ret[
which, with excessive modesty on their part, had b[
concealed from us until then.

This honest tale of fisherman's luck is told for the sa[
the dual moral which it conveys,—namely, as a rule, d[
trust the word of a Boniface of the woods as to where [
good fishing is, if it happens to be beyond the range of [
dinner-horn, and don't employ a "hotel guide" if you [
help it. The "independent guides" have a reputation [
make and keep, and their employment depends upon [
but a man paid by a hotel keeper so much for the sea[
prefers whittling under the wood-shed to rowing and rou[
ing it, for the same money.

Our two New York friends had enough of that sor[
delusion, and departed in high dudgeon the next morn[
for Paul Smith's. The Editor and I remained, resolved[
spite of our chagrin and disgust, to test still further [
possibilities of the fishing, and to enjoy at least the cha[
ing scenery.

CHAPTER IX.

A few days after, taking two of the best guides, "Chris," and Halsey, we made an expedition down the outlet to the Still-water. Providing ourselves with two days' provisions, guns and fishing tackle, we set forth with a faith and expectancy quite childlike in its simplicity, considering our recent experience.

Rowing down the outlet to the rapids we left our boats, shouldered our packs, and made the carry of a mile and a half or more below the rapids, where we found two other boats which we speedily converted to our own use. We had reached the Still-water, which extends (with the exception of one-fourth of a mile of rapids) six or seven miles, and into which flow many small, cold streams. At the mouths of these the trout congregate in the months of July and August, when they greedily take the fly. We had come upon a charming region. Our descent down the river on that quiet, peaceful July day revealed to us the true beauties of the Adirondacks. Success rewarded our fishing, and many a hungry trout leaped up to our flies as they hovered an instant and then settled upon the water where the cool brooks entered the main stream. One hardly knew which delight to choose—the gaze upon the winding river and forest shores, or the skillful cast, and the leap, play and capture of the gamy trout. To tell the truth, we chose both, and with such absorbing interest that it was well into the afternoon before we sought a mossy bank, under shady trees, by a cool spring, and dined.

The guides respected our hunger, and the beautiful trout curled and browned before the fire until they were food fit for a Roman Emperor. A spring bubbled at our feet, the merciful smudge startled and awed the vengeful, winged hosts that gathered to dine on us, we ate our fill, and then the aroma of the pipe,—the hunter's solace and the fisherman's comfort,—mingled its fragrance with the breath of spruce and balsam and the mossy bank on which we reclined. There are days,—and there are days. This was of the sort to be looked forward to, enjoyed like choicest friendship, and remembered like strains of music that go to the heart.

Again we were on the water, floating down the river and enticing the river's game as before. The evening approached. The guides took one of the boats and went a little way up-stream to build a camp for the night, leaving us in the other boat to fish at our leisure. Suddenly the sky darkened, and we discovered the approach of a thunder-storm, black and savage. We hastened up the river to find our camp, and in a little bay, or inlet, saw the boat of our guides, pulled our own on shore, turned it over, and bestowed our luggage under it to keep it dry.

Drawing on our rubber coats, just as the big rain-drops began to descend, we hurried up to the thick growth of small spruces, where our guides were working with might and main to build a brush camp. The rain came down in sheets, in torrents, in floods,—descended without method, —deluged us; while we for a time sought protection under the dripping branches of our half-completed shelter. The trees trickled and then poured water and were full of showers; the moss under our feet was like a saturated sponge, oozy wet; there was not a dry stick or limb for a fire,—not even the lee-side of a big tree for shelter,—" water, water, everywhere," and not the slightest suspicion that there would ever again be a dry place in that region. We stood about in our slouched-hats and rubber coats, as helpless, bedraggled and dispirited as ever did a community of barn yard fowls in an autumnal rain.

The night was near at hand. The pressing questions were: when will this flood cease? where shall we sleep and what shall be our bed? how shall we kindle a fire in this drowned and water-soaked forest?

The Editor is a man of keen perceptions and quick decision. After a word with me, he said:

"Boys, how far is it to Fuller's?"

"Ten miles—rapids, carries and all."

"Going to rain all night?"

"Guess so."

"Can you take us through and home in the dark?"

"That we can;"—and it was Chris. Crandall who spoke, the most noted guide of the region,—tall, bony, shaggy, *one-legged* and using a crutch and cane, rude and rough, but with a commanding intellect that made him the favorite hunter and guide of all that part of the wilderness, and his word law with all his associates.

"Then we'll go;"—and in the pouring rain we stowed our luggage and ourselves into the boats, and started on our toilsome way up-stream in search of a roof and a dry bed. Still the rain poured, as we proceeded up the river to the rapids, down which we had bumped and thumped, but up which there was to be some vigorous tugging.

The Editor has a manly form that holds a wagon-seat down firmly, ballasts a boat satisfactorily, and affords an exhaustive test of the honest materials and workmanship of Fairbanks' scales. It accorded with the fitness of things that on this occasion Chris., into whose two arms had gone the strength of the lost leg, should be his oarsman, while the tough, wiry little Halsey should row his slim and thin companion. But at the rapids, Chris. was at a disadvantage. He could tramp through the forest with the best of us. He could carry a small pack on his back. He could leap a log with his crutch and cane and one leg where our two legs faltered,—but he couldn't wade up rapids among the rocks and swirls, in a thunder-storm, and at the same time drag a boat behind him.

The Editor could, and he did. Ensconced in a huge, black rubber coat and under a broad-brimmed, slouch-hat, he preserved a semblance of dryness and comfort in the upper story, but the basement was hopelessly damp. With a rope over his shoulder he did good mule-power work at towing the boat, as he picked his way among the hidden rocks, and splashed and pitched and stumbled his devious course up the rapids,—following, it is true, the lead of Chris., who forged ahead like a locomotive under full steam. Meanwhile, the slim passenger was reaping the benefit of thinness and conservative avoirdupois; for Halsey insisted on seating him on the luggage in the middle of the boat, "to keep it dry" he said, while he, the kind-hearted little fellow, pushed and pulled the boat up-stream. However, the situation was only moistly satisfactory, for the rain let down fearfully, but didn't let up a bit.

The Editor, half the time up to his knees in the water beneath, while the waters above poured in streams from hat and coat, looked back appreciatively upon the triumphal progress I was making;—and I saw through the rain, by the humor in his eye and the comedy all over his face, that he fully comprehended both the humidity and the humor of the situation.

And Chris.,—it was rough comedy for his one leg and crutch and cane. He couldn't even contemplate the satisfaction there would be in telling the story of this tramp up the rapids,—it would be such an old story. Yet he could joke, even in the river, among the rocks and pouring rain, —but such jokes! They were Titanic,—belching like a volcano,—the thumps of Thor's hammer,—thunderous,— and I am sorry to say, in connection with this sweet picture, profane as the Devil—or Prometheus, if he swore. It was apparent that Chris., after all, preferred dry land for his one leg to tramp on, and that it was not so much consolation as the mathematics of the case would suggest, that in wading he only wet one foot while other men must wet two.

But it was over at last,—this passage up the rapids,—and

we swung along up the Still-Water again, by legitimate methods of water-travel, content, even, to let it rain, if we could only have the water smooth as well as wet.

As we proceeded, my boat being in advance, we saw a deer standing, broadside towards us, in the shallow water at the margin of the stream, and looking intently at us. Halsey seized the gun, which lay by his side, aimed, pulled the trigger, and the cap (suffering from the general depression and dampness) snapped. Whereat the deer leisurely walked out of the stream, daintily lifting his feet out of the water as he went, and disappeared in the thick underbrush. I was mortified that our appearance inspired no more terror in the beast, and felt that it was not even beastly complimentary. Halsey fumbled in his vest-pocket for a fresh cap, while the deer was walking off, but was at least half a minute too late in preparing his weapon for discharge. I have no doubt a deer, if consulted, would recommend all hunters to use a muzzle-loader.

Scarcely fifteen minutes had elapsed before we saw another deer feeding in the water. It seemed a good day for deer. The rain had just ceased and the last rays of the setting sun were slanting up-stream. We were out of range, and Halsey leveling his gun took good aim, while I, in a highly excited state of mind, seated in the stern of the boat, paddled, pushed and somehow advanced eight or ten rods to, almost, within ten rods of the deer. He looked up, and, conscious I have no doubt that a dry cap had been put upon the gun, or perhaps imagining that our generally bedraggled appearance was only a blind and that we were after all valiant and dangerous, leisurely turned to depart. At that instant Halsey pulled the trigger and the old muzzle-loader roared and volleyed like a round half dozen thunder-bolts. There was a great splashing and dashing of water for a moment. We thought the lively animal was down and that all we now had to do was to advance in good order and pick up our game. But as the smoke lifted we saw, to our dismay, the creature spring ashore with two or three vigorous bounds and disappear. Scarcely had we realized what had occurred, when, a few rods above, this deer or another ran across the stream to the opposite shore and plunged into the thicket.

"Great guns!" said I, "Halsey, is this country full of deer?"

"Well, I can't say about that," replied he, "but I do think what there are of 'em are about the liveliest fellows I ever did see! Just think of it, now! This old gun was loaded with buck-shot to kill. That chap must have got some of 'em under his skin. I wouldn't have given ten cents to be insured on him—I'd 'ave bet my last dollar that he was mine. And to think that in less than a minute he or another fellow hove in sight! It's mighty queer." And the guide relapsed into a mournful, meditative silence.

Chris. now approached and insisted that he had plainly seen the buck-shot strike the water, falling short of the aim, and that these caused the splashing and not the deer. However, both guides went ashore and searched for blood, but it was now growing dark and if there were such traces they were unable to discover them.

The truth of history requires me to add that before we reached the long carry, the Editor and Chris. saw still another deer, and that after we had taken our boats above the bridge and before we reached the lake, in the darkness, we drove out two more that "whistled" and fled away,— making five or six that we saw or heard that evening. Nobody in the region was able to inform me whether any lone and solitary boatman had ever been attacked and trampled to death by these wandering herds. It is well, however, to go down that river well armed.

Soon after the deer's adventure with us, (it didn't exactly seem to be our adventure, under the circumstances,) we came to a shingle-maker's deserted, little bark-shanty. In the fast waning light we went ashore, and while lunching stretched our weary limbs in the only dry place we had seen since the storm broke upon us. We left our bag of potatoes and some other provisions, for the next party that might make an expedition here. The old woodsmen are accustomed to make these impromptu *caches*, and invariably, when reaching a deserted camp, hunt about to find something that may have been left by any party preceding them. A half-peck of potatoes is always an acceptable "find," and a few lemons are gratefully appreciated, while a piece of fat pork hid under the bark-roof is not despised. Genuine food in the wilderness, with the nearest provision store twenty miles away, and the stock on hand reduced to low ebb, is prized like water in the desert.

When we started out for our long tramp over the carry it was dark on the river, but the forest was blackness itself, while the occasionally renewed rain-fall added to the general unpleasantness of the situation. We pushed, as we thought, for the trail. After struggling through underbrush and fallen trees awhile Chris. hesitated, went this way and that, while we stood still awaiting developments. He finally said, "I don't believe I know where that path is!" Then he plunged—one leg, crutch, cane and all—into the deeper darkness, and we followed as well as we could, looking hither and thither for some sign of a trail. Then we halted. Even the valiant and skilful old woodsman, of many years' experience, was evidently lost. I ventured to suggest that the shanty was at least dry and would make us comfortable until morning.

"I don't believe we can find that, now," said Chris.; "I'm blamed if I haven't lost all my reckoning, it's so confounded dark. I'll make one more trial, and if I don't strike the trail we'll get back to the river, somehow, and hunt up the shanty and wait for day-light. Just stand still, all of you, while I make a circuit around here. When I call, you answer me, so's I can tell where I'm going to."

We stood as directed, and the veteran disappeared. For a time we heard him crashing through the underbrush and fallen limbs, and swearing away to his heart's content, until he passed out of hearing. We waited several minutes to hear his call, but pride in his woodcraft restrained him, or his not altogether reverent soliloquy pre-occupied him. Fearing he would wander off beyond the sound of our voices, we called and called again, but no response came. We were really alarmed for his safety.

But finally, at a good round distance, we heard his gruff voice, raised to a high key, shouting, "Here's the road! Come over here!" We responded as quickly as we could, following his voice as he occasionally called, and at length found the trail.

Halsey lighted up the jack,—I don't know why he didn't do so before,—which enabled us to see our path. From this time on, until we reached our boats, away we went, Chris. leading the procession and Halsey with the jack immediately after, at a break-neck pace. Chris. walked as if he had four legs, and we, with only a pair apiece, found difficulty in keeping up with him.

It was eleven o'clock at night when we reached the Meacham Lake House,—wet, pretty cold from our ride on the lake, thoroughly tired,—but with a dry bed to sleep in, and a roof to cover us—two things which sundry forest experiences have taught me to highly prize. There is glory in "roughing it," but there is a vast deal of comfort, when night comes, in having some place to lay your head where the rain comes not, and the waters do not break through and dampen.

When we came to think of it by day-light, in dry clothes, and our joints limbered up, we rejoiced that we had seen Still-water, the pleasant, winding river, and the forest scenery,—common enough in the Adirondacks, but ever new and ever enticing to the lover of untamed nature. Not the least of its attractiveness lies in the fact that it is out of the beaten path in the wilderness, and of the flowing tides of tourists who annually pour through the popular thoroughfares of the great forest, and pass by and leave this secluded stream to the adventurous sportsman.

CHAPTER X.

One day our hostess dimly saw the bottom of the flour barrel. Fuller's steeds,—having a vouched-for record of three and a half miles an hour,—were harnessed up, and "Jimmy," the Irish lad, was given the ribbons and a lengthy memorandum, with orders to proceed to Malone with all dispatch that day, and to return the next with edibles and edibles. The Editor, mindful of his sanctum, and with visions before his eyes of the irate subscriber who should demand that his paper be stopped if the editors were all going a-fishing, seized this opportunity and departed from the wilderness.

I remained. I had had a little controversy with my doctor who ordered me out of town and into the woods. I had been informed that I possessed "vocal chords,"—and that a month in the Adirondacks would restore their wonted, harmonious vibrations. If you have "vocal chords," it is best to get rid of them, or, as I did, go a-fishing and forget them for good and all. However, as the Editor departed, I put on metaphorical widow's weeds for the space of an entire day and then warmed over my affections and fixed them firmly upon a younger and a handsomer,—the Young Man from Brooklyn.

The days went on with quiet lounging on the grass under the pine trees in front of the house, the pretty lake in full view; or, with tramps to little gems of lakes hid in the forest within easy distance. One day we cleared a path through the underbrush to a bluff on the lake-shore, and on a mossy-grassy spot erected a tent under the trees, which became a great resort for the ladies and the toddling wee ones. There was famous rifle-shooting at sundry bottles put upon a stake out in the lake. A morning surprise came now and then, as a fat buck hung upon a limb near the house, the result of the night's jack-hunting. Fishing parties and tourists were coming and going, bringing and carrying out mail. A new sail-boat had to be tested. All together, there was a world of enjoyment of things hardly worthy to tell, but very delightful to do.

There had been, at one time, a notable accession to our numbers. The Sheriff of the county came, convoying a party of schoolma'ams who desired here to divert their minds and restore their freshness during some portion of their vacation. I surrendered my room to the schoolma'ams, and temporarily took another on the ground floor with the Sheriff as my room-mate. That personage was a bachelor, but exceedingly thin, as if the cares of a large family had worn him down, or his ancestors on the Mayflower had contracted constitutional and ineradicable dyspepsia on the long voyage to Plymouth Rock. He looked all the thinner for being very tall and having high cheek-bones, a long neck, and a preponderating Adam's apple.

On a Sunday morning, two or three days after the new arrangement was inaugurated, when I arose,—the spirit of civilization in me stimulated by the presence, in the immediate neighborhood, of the schoolma'ams,—I faithfully applied the razor to my own not excessively rounded face. The Sheriff, sitting on the edge of the bed, thoughtfully engaged in pulling on his stockings, watched the operation with interest. Then I saw, by the reflection in the diminutive mirror, that he rubbed his chin and hollow cheeks and looked for a moment meditatively down upon the piece of rag-carpet at his feet.

"I wish I was shaved," he at length said, in a melancholy tone, and added despairingly, "but I never shaved myself in all my life, and I don't suppose there is anybody here that could shave me."

Something in the sad face—perhaps it was its grizzliness —moved me, and I cheeringly remarked:

"Oh, it isn't very difficult; I think you can do it; and you are welcome to the use of my razor, if you want to try."

"No, I never can,—I should be sure to cut myself all to pieces;" and the Sheriff sighed as he rubbed his chin again, and felt that it was wholly unpresentable, and remembered that it was Sunday, and the schoolma'ams would meet him at the breakfast table.

There was a long pause. Then he looked piteously up at me, as I was adjusting my neck-tie, and hesitatingly said:

"If it wouldn't be asking too much, would you—might I ask you—do you suppose you could shave me?"

"Well," said I, "I suppose I can try; but I'm awfully

afraid I'll make a bad job of it; and I might cut you horribly."

With a sigh of commingled desperation and relief, the Sheriff replied:

"If you'll try it, I'll take the risk."

With a face that had to be kept long, because it twitched with suppressed laughter, I proceeded to the tonsorial task. I planted him in a chair squarely before the window, lathered his face until the whole rugged surface looked like a *meringue;* and girding myself for the labor *not* put down as one of the labors of Hercules, I seized his nose in the most approved fashion—and scraped. My victim winced.

"Does it hurt?"

"Some—but go on—I can stand it."

I scraped again, and the blood oozed through the sallow skin.

"I have to bear on, you see," I said, "for this razor isn't in the best order."

"Go ahead!" came through the shut teeth.

Whether the Sheriff was pale or not, I couldn't see, for the lather. And whether the eyes were blood-shot did not appear, for they were closed in determined resignation.

I found I was in for it, and worked away with might and main. There were few more words,—the time for them was passed. I scraped again and again, and the blood oozed from every freshly-shaven surface. It was my turn to be desperate. Suppose I should utterly ruin the Sheriff's face! What if I made him totally unpresentable for a week! This was no Jericho where he could tarry until his beard should grow, for the schoolma'ams were *here!* And then came the temptation to make a slash or two at the Adam's apple and end the whole business. I was becoming nervous, and my whole body was quivering with suppressed nervous laughter. I wanted to scream and throw the razor out of the window, and jump out after it.

"For Heaven's sake, go on, get through!" groaned the Sheriff.

That broke the spell, and I fell to work again with more coolness. I reached the hollow cheeks; I had carefully gone over the sharp chin, the long jaw-bones, and high cheek-bones,—leaving my "mark," it is true, here and there well cut in,—with tolerable success, from my point of view, and considering my education and opportunities in the businesss. But now I had come to the most critical piece of work before me. How to go down into the hollows with a straight-bladed instrument with an awkward handle like a razor's, nearly posed me. I meditated thrusting my fingers into the Sheriff's cheeks to plump them out, but was afraid he was by this time mad enough to bite me, or that I might cut through and slash my own fingers. I can't to this day quite imagine how I accomplished it, but I did somehow, shave out the hollows, with only a few small slices being taken off on the surrounding ridges. I suppose in times of great excitement or danger we are inspired to our best, and no subsequent effort of memory can recall precisely the mental processes of those moments of inspired activity. That is my case exactly in regard to that last and supreme effort in shaving the Sheriff.

I finished. Applying a damp towel to the scene of my activities, my work in all its sculpturesque effects was revealed to my gaze. I trembled as I thought of the inevitable moment when it should be revealed by the mirror to the Sheriff himself.

"There! its done,—and done just as well as I know how!" said I, with a carefully tempered tone of self-vindication.

"Oh!" sighed the Sheriff, as he opened his eyes, lifted his hand to his face, and gazed into the mirror,—"but I —I thank you!"

That was the only time I ever shaved a Sheriff.

CHAPTER XI.

On the whole, Fuller's furnished a variety of entertainment, and was enjoyable. But the most delightful of places and the most charming of experiences become monotonous after a time, and, a favorable opportunity offering, one day I joined a party of ladies and gentlemen and departed from Meacham Lake to Paul Smith's. Our flotilla of boats went down the lake to the rapids, we walked to the bridge, and there were met by teams sent up from Smith's.

The ride through the woods was rather rough, but reasonably comfortable for a wood's road, until we reached " Burnt Ground, " where the road became excellent. Here was a large, tree-less, stump-less section of several hundred acres, supposed to have been swept by fire at some period long past. A feeble settlement of a dozen or fifteen families maintains the struggle for existence in the centre of this tract, the men cultivating a few acres of the sandy soil, hunting, trapping and fishing, and, as occasion offers, acting as guides for sportsmen among the little lakes that lie in clusters on every side in the forest. The notable man of this out-of-the-world hamlet is A. C. McCollum, a kindly old gentleman who came hither from the great world outside, after a succession of domestic bereavements which almost broke his heart, but left him even more kindly and gentle than before. Little bare-footed children were running about upon the stunted grass, or peering at us from behind their modest mothers in the doorways, as we passed, while the humble school-house gave evidence that even here the American idea of education was not forgotten. The men looked honest and sincere, but sad, I thought, as if, after all, this life of poverty and seclusion was far from satisfying.

Passing this peculiar and exceptional feature of the wilderness, we were again among the trees, climbing and descending hills where the forest growth was sparse, or in the midst of heavy timber,—sometimes crossing streams, and skirting lakelets and the more ambitious waters, Osgood Pond and Barnum's Pond. At one point we came upon a group of tall Norway spruces that looked like importations indeed. At another, we passed the borders of a tamarack swamp, notable as the place where many a deer had been stealthily hunted and shot. In the sandy road-way we saw the fresh, clear-cut tracks of a doe and her fawn.

Suddenly, among the trees appeared a telegraph pole, and another, and a single wire stretched between, and we wheeled into a travel-worn road along which the telegraph line ran,—the most startling symbol of civilization that one could come upon in the wilderness. We followed this line a mile or less, and drew up in front of a spacious and imposing hotel.—Paul Smith's. Had this dropped, a palace, from the skies? Were we waking, or dreaming? Whence came all these fastidiously dressed men and women and children? The entire picture presented was a marvel to one for many days a dweller at the quiet little log-house on

Meacham Lake, and accustomed to evenings at the rude guide-house.

"Paul Smith's" is familiar to thousands of summer tourists who "take it in" along with Newport, Long Branch and Saratoga, as well as to those veterans of the angle and the hunt, who for many years have annually resorted hither, making this the base from which to project excursions into the deeper wilderness, there to dwell in camp and tent and pursue in solitude the pleasures of the pathless woods, the limpid lakes and winding streams.

The hotel stands upon a bluff looking southward out upon Lower St. Regis Lake, beyond which lie Spitfire and Upper St. Regis. It is a long, four-story, wooden edifice, with a broad verandah along its entire front, and capable of accommodating a hundred guests. The guide-house, on the shore of the lake and to the right, is a long, two-story frame building, used below for housing seventy-five to one hundred trim, light and shapely boats. Above it is converted into sleeping and living rooms for the guides engaged by Mr. Smith for the season. A bowling-alley still further away, and frame barns, shops and an ice-house complete this really remarkable hostelry and its appurtenances. An excellent road, traversed daily by a stage-coach, leads out by way of Bloomingdale and Ausable Forks to the rail-road terminus at Point of Rocks, whence the tourist journeys by rail to Plattsburg and whither he will. The "click" of the telegraph, in the hotel-office, assures you that you are no longer cut off from mankind, and you suddenly come to realize that you may forthwith, if you will, have a chat with your wife and babies at home.

Something else comes to you,—knowledge of good and evil—as to your attire. After weeks of life out of the reach of daily mails and the instantaneous telegram, you have become as unconscious of your outer covering as a tortoise is of his shell. It fits and protects you, and what more is to be desired? The first five minutes over, at Paul Smith's, and in the privacy of your room, you dive into your knapsack for the fig-leaves. Alas, you have become conscious; your freedom is gone; you have in effect come back to town; and Tom, Dick and Harry salute you on the street, and you know that they know whether you are "dressed" or not. For the hour, the genuine, careless joy of the woodsman in you is dead.

When evening comes at Paul Smith's, the long parlor is brilliantly lighted. At the piano is seated a lady in elegant summer costume, and at her masterful touch the rich tones rise and swell and sink and die away in music. By her side, turning the sheets, as she plays, stand men of faultless attire and foreign speech. Ladies and gentlemen walk up and down the room, and pretty children, fastidiously dressed, romp and frolic with the irrepressible freedom of childhood.

There are social games, sober family gatherings and flirtations in the nooks and corners, and in the office letter-writing and newspaper reading. The fishermen and hunters who came in, from every direction, before tea, in their fancy hunting costumes reäppear in Scotch and broadcloth and linen, only their brown faces revealing to you that they are genuine sportsmen.

Meanwhile, the long, broad veranda is crowded with easy chairs, and the fragrant Havana mingles its perfume with the aroma of balsam and spruce and pine floating ever in over the cooling waters of the St. Regis. Here is a knot of respectful and credulous listeners assembled around a rotund and enthusiastic Doctor of Divinity from New York, who is telling fishing stories that draw heavily upon the faith of his hearers, and of deer-hunts in which he figured as the hero, out-Murraying Murray. But it is vastly interesting, for the learned Doctor tells a story well, and you choose to believe that he is essentially telling the honest truth,—as his memory sees it.

Other knots of men are gathered all along the veranda, and their talk is of the woods and lakes and streams, of trout and deer.

On the grass in front, is a jolly guide playing with a little child, tossing it up, rolling it over on the turf, laughing, and as happy as a fond papa can be; and well he may be happy, for he has this evening just returned with two tourists, after eleven days' absence, during which he has made the grand circuit to John Brown's Tract by one chain of lakes and streams, and returned by another. His wife and a baby, and the end of his hard trip, have given him joy enough to-night to make up for many a backache on the long carries.

At ten o'clock every body goes to bed. It is both the fashion and the inclination.

There was one learned old Doctor and Professor from New Haven who interested me very much. He was quite infirm, and his son, who accompanied him, with filial devotion anticipated every want. The brave old man was out early every morning, and, with a guide, rowed around the little rocky peninsula, south-easterly from the hotel, to the mouth of a cold stream that comes through the tamaracks into the lake not far beyond. There, at the edge of the lily-pads (successors of those noted by W. C. Prime in his delicious volume, "I Go A Fishing," on page 125) he skilfully and patiently cast his flies until he took the one big trout awaiting his morning call, and then returned to the hotel to breakfast and for the day.

It was something more than a splendid trout that he brought to our view as we met him at the landing. The young heart in the old body,—the genuine enthusiasm of the veteran angler,— the glorification of the gentle art which has soothed and comforted many an aged philosopher,—all this he revealed to us, and we wanted to lift the grand old man to our shoulders and bear him in reverent triumph up the ascent.

Another day, a robust, handsome, middle-aged gentleman, who they said was a wealthy, hard-working merchant, of New York City, went early in the morning, with his guide, to Osgood Pond. In the early evening they returned, the guide bringing, literally, a big back-load of the finest trout I ever saw,—great, splendid fellows, all that the man could comfortably carry. There was admiration and rejoicing on all hands, and especially, among the ladies. I was delighted that the triumph belonged to this splendid specimen of the robust gentleman whom I had admired for his manly beauty and pure, good face; and I put his picture by the side of that of the young-old Doctor, in my memories of Paul Smith's and St. Regis.

There is a charming ramble, out among the trees, east of the house, and thence all over the wooded, rocky peninsula jutting into the lake. One may sit and lounge on the rocks at the water's edge and look out upon the lake and see how prettily the breezes play with the wavelets; or gaze beyond, and watch the summit of St. Regis Mountain, noting what a world of blue there is in the atmosphere when it rests upon a mountain's brow; or let the eye wander far and near upon the forest, and dream and dream again of the procession of the centuries that have come and gone, while the forest, ever changing, yet remains ever the same. There are a hundred things one may do, at such a resort as Paul Smith's, besides fishing, that will be both delightful to the tired mind and delicious to all the senses. I confess that, while there, I enjoyed these un-sportsmanlike things to the utmost.

CHAPTER XII.

But, after a time, I longed for some little adventure. The life I had been leading in the woods, although easy and half indolent, in the main, had put vigor and health in my blood and frame, and I fairly ached to "let myself out," for once, before I should return to the work-a-day life that awaited me outside of the wilderness.

The opportunity came, one morning, when a tourist and his guide started out upon the popular excursion to Martin's by way of the Saranacs. They cheerfully consented that I should accompany them as far as I desired, to return alone when I should choose. Selecting a light, trim, Adirondack boat, when they set out I followed them, plying the oars with an ease that surprised me. The flabbiness of muscle belonging to the man of sedentary habits had given place to sinewy strength. With swinging stroke we crossed the lower St. Regis Lake, wound and twisted our way through the inlet to Spitfire Pond, and so on to and through Upper St. Regis, to the landing at the foot of the carry to Big Clear Pond. The guide, as we went along, pointed out various land-marks by which I would be enabled, on my return, to find the streams connecting the different lakes,—particularly calling my attention to seven dead pines near the outlet of Upper St. Regis. It would seem a very easy matter to find the outlet or inlet of a lake, but it is, in fact, exceedingly difficult. The bays and coves and points are all delusive, and the stream you seek generally steals in or out obscurely, at some unexpected angle, hardly making a sign of its presence until you are right upon it. I had learned so much before, and now I noted every land-mark closely, conscious that any failure to recall these might result, on my return, in an all-night's solitary, supperless and tentless bivouac on a mosquito-infested shore.

Leaving my boat at the landing, I went over to St. Germain's, on Big Clear Pond, a carry of two miles over which the St. Germain—or, "Sangemo"—boys draw boats and luggage on a rude sled, with a very thin horse. The walk is easy and agreeable through the woods, and quite a relief after sitting long in a boat. The St. Germain family consists chiefly of the father, a little old black-eyed, shock-headed, voluble Canadian-Frenchman, and his wife and three or four grown up boys who look as if they had never been quite tamed. They are great hunters,—and have been known to do close shooting, under imagined provocation, at something not properly coming under the head of game, except in a cannibal country. They had several hungry and whining hounds tied and penned up, but no other wild animals, although a deer or a bear is generally among the few attractions they offer to strangers.

We were met here by a party of two gentlemen and two handsome ladies and three or four little children, with their guides, who were on their way from the Saranacs to

Paul's. It was a right merry party, and they laughed and chatted and drank St. Germain's "pop-beer" with a charming air of confidence in its integrity,—as delighted with every thing as if they were enjoying an after-theater lunch at Delmonico's. The last we saw of them they were setting off, ladies, children and all, on their two-mile walk over the carry, with light, tripping steps and the merriest laughter, as if walking down the lawn at home, after tea, for a boat ride on the river.

This was not quite the sort of sunshine and romance one would be looking out for on a carry, but it is precisely the thing not uncommon on these forest thoroughfares among the St. Regis and Saranac waters,—a region which has charms of its own for the gentler sex and all others who want to see the woods and waters in their primitive state, with "improvements." The sportsman is crowded, every year, into remoter regions; but there is room enough for him, and he ought not to grudge some little portion of his realm to beauty and childhood. He must, however, heed the "move on," which the increasing multitudes utter all along his favorite haunts. If he is a sensible, generous and gentle-hearted sportsman, he will not grumble at this and talk of "Murray's fools," but will rejoice that it is possible for so many to share with him the forest and its benefits to health and heart. The unexplored wilderness is close at hand, and it is his if he will but seize it. Let the wife and children journey over, and enjoy, the favorite old ways, even if their presence frightens the deer to remoter regions and the trout are to be sought in more secluded haunts.

After a brief rest, I procured another boat, and, still following my companions, rowed through Big Clear Pond to the carry leading to the head of the Upper Saranac. This is a "draw-carry" four miles long, a solid road over which both boats and tourists are transported on wagons through the forest. Two or three houses in the midst of small clearings are on the shore, and by dint of loud hallooing on the part of the guide, before we reached land, we called a man and team to the landing. Again I left my boat, while my companions had theirs loaded upon the wagon, and we all got aboard and proceeded in great state and comfort to the hotel at the head of the Upper Saranac Lake, where we arrived at noon.

"Cox's" is a two-story, frame house, much less pretentious than Paul Smith's, capable, however, of accommodating sixty guests, which it did the night before our arrival. It is situated in a cleared, grass-grown space, of several acres,—a high and dry, sandy plateau, at least fifteen feet above the level of the lake. The southerly view from the verandah, upon the lake and mountains, south and east, is very fine and impressive, and is deservedly noted. White Face Mountain can be seen distinctly, and Mt. Marcy is brought into view by going down the lake a little distance. The lake is one of the largest in the wilderness.

The junior partner of the firm of Cox & Lewis, then conducting the hotel, very kindly rowed me down the lake several miles, before dinner, and I returned to the hotel with the impression that I had been shown one of the grandest parts of the water system of the Adirondacks,

The mountain region must always bear off the heroic honors, but the Upper Saranac, in my opinion, contends with the Raquette for the milder supremacy of beauty and grandeur combined.

At dinner, I sat near a husband and wife,—the husband, an invalid who came too late to the health-giving forest. He was as brown as sun and wind could make one,—the result of many weeks of out-door life,—but so thin and weak that the complexion of health was a wretched satire and mockery. His wife was as tender and solicitous as if he had been her infant child; but he answered her inquiries in a hollow voice that was startling and painful to hear. He leaned his head on his hand and his elbow on the table and pushed aside his plate of food, unable to eat, with a look of despair on his face, as if, at last, he had given up his brave, long fight for life and had resolved to struggle no longer. He was a stranger,—I saw him only a few minutes,—but I have imagined a hundred times the sorrowful details of his summer's endeavor to arrest the progress of insidious disease, and wondered, and wondered again, if he lived to reach his home, and if he died with his family at his bed-side. This man's hollow, sun-browned face and despairing look, and his wife's anxious brow were the saddest sight I ever happened upon in the wilderness.

The cloud of the Saranac Hotel was obscuring the sunshine of the scene at St. Germain's Carry; and I finished my dinner as speedily as my appetite and good manners would permit, and joined more joyous society on the lawn in front of the house. That sorrow was not my burden to bear.

My return to Paul Smith's, alone, that afternoon, secured to me a "time record" which gave me a day's distinction, and which, I presume, "Charley" Martin, Paul's brother-in-law and chief manager and useful man in general, remembers to this day; and I expect him to vouch for it.

I left the Saranac House at three o'clock, walked the four-mile carry in fifty-seven minutes; rowed through a heavy sea across Big Clear Pond, about four miles, in thirty-five minutes; then rested, at St. Germain's, twenty-five minutes; walked the two-mile carry in half an hour, and rowed through Upper St. Regis, and the connecting streams, four miles, in forty minutes, to Paul Smith's,—and that evening walked the verandah half an hour, with a friend I found there, for exercise! Thanks to the woods for that!

I think my story staggered some of the guides, but "Charley," whose guest I was, believed it—at least, he did not venture anything to the contrary. I here re-affirm it, —and appeal to the country!

My halt at St. Germain's gave me an opportunity to interview the old Frenchman. I opened his heart with a liberal portion of the contents of my tobaco-pouch, and with a dime or two unlocked—what I found still more comforting—his wife's pantry, whence she produced very respectable doughnuts and cheese. The old man and I smoked together, some time, and he talked volubly; but, for the life of me, I could understand only a few of his words, although I caught their woodsy and fishy spirit well enough. The half-tamed boys were conquered by the same means, and congratulated me on my successful voyage through the rough sea of Big Clear;—but the genuineness of their wonder at and admiration of my exploit may have been established by my prompt and liberal payment for the use of their boat brought safe to the landing. If I had been drowned, I should have been more troublesome and less profitable to them.

At the other end of the carry from St. Germain's, I encountered a party of Harvard College boys on their way to Long Lake. They were without guides, and carried their boats and luggage and cooking utensils on their backs and shoulders, after the fashion of men trained in the woods rather than on a college campus. They were in fine spirits, but were anticipating a long pull and hard work before they should reach their camp, where they were to be met by companions who had preceeded them.

The next day I found myself none the worse for my trip to the Upper Saranac, and planned to make the ascent of St. Regis Mountain; but the atmosphere was very smoky, and I abandoned the project. This is one of the expeditions every man and every strong-minded and limbed lady at Paul Smith's is expected to make. A fat gentleman, who sat next to me at the breakfast table, had made it the day before. He had forgotten to carry up with him a bottle of water, and had suffered almost intolerably from thirst. The climbing up the rocks, moreover, had bruised and fatigued him greatly; and he declared with spirited emphasis that the whole thing was a "horrible job," and he wouldn't repeat it if you would give him all the mountains you could see from the top of St. Regis.

One of the prettiest pictures seen at Paul Smith's, is when, after sunset, a dozen or a score of boats filled with ladies and children, push out upon the lake,—each boat gracefully rowed by a strong oarsman who knows how to row a genuine Adirondack boat with swiftness, and handle it with safety. Indeed, the commingling there of gayety and sobriety, fashion and simplicity, sportsman's life and social life, excites constant interest in the mind of a "looker-on in Venice" as I was. It is not what one goes to the wilderness for, but for all that it is delightful to see all these people so happy in the woods, and especially the little folks.

Having, at length, lingered and lounged and dreamed away my allotted time at this famous resort, I sought an opportunity to retrace my steps to Meacham, and thence out, to Malone and home. It came, one deliciously fresh and dewy morning; and, with their cheerful assent, I joined a party of sportsmen and their guides, going to Meacham outlet to camp—the "Still-water" where the Editor and I experienced the earlier sensations of the victims of the Deluge.

The luggage was deposited in a big, strong, lumber wagon, provided with a rack upon which were placed two boats, side-by-side and bottom upwards. On these we sat, while the road was good, but found much comfort, at times, in walking. One of the gentlemen was a young Reverend, who had conscientiously saved a hundred dollars from his meager salary as a pastor, for a month in the woods. He loved the wilderness, its mountains, lakes and streams, with an ardent devotion, and was as genial, robust and gentle as becomes a true disciple of the rod. He fondled his rifle as if that, too, was a part of his dreaming while he was saving his hundred dollars. I did not doubt that he preached and taught all the more wisely for his accustomed month with nature and the benignant lessons she teaches her true votaries. His companion was an incipient Yale Freshman, to whose youthful spirits the air of the woods was like wine, without the headache.

Our ways diverged at McCollum's, at Burnt Ground, and I parted with my companions, with a powerful yearning to accompany them to camp and enjoy with them what they had in store. It was here and now that I made the acquaintance of McCollum and learned, from his lips, his sad history of the domestic sorrow which brought him hither. Yet he was so strong and gentle, so manly in every sense, that I felt I was in the presence of one who had indeed learned to "suffer and be strong."

He sent me with his horses and driver to the Meacham Lake House, whither we drove, at a break-neck speed, over rocks and stumps and roots, while I held to my seat in momentary expectation of a general smash as complete, to all intents and purposes, as a rail-road collision. But horses and wagons, in the woods, all seem to be made upon honor, and we went through to our destination with nothing worse than a terrible shaking-up.

The out-going party which I had hoped to intercept, had gone. However, on the following day, I caught a ride to "Woodford's"—an old sportsmen's hotel in the borders of the forest—where I procured a horse and wagon, and reached Malone in the evening. The gas-lights in the streets were burning, the solid pavements were under my feet,—and I, loyally as I love the woods, must admit that, after my lengthy sojourn in the wilderness, these, and the rows of blocks and solid buildings, gave me great satisfaction and a new appreciation of the comforts and pleasures of the works of man.

The next morning came in holiday attire. I met it half way, by discarding every vestige of my clothing worn in the woods, with its smell of smoke and tar-oil, found a barber, and felt that my wanderings in the forests for that summer were ended. I was again in the land of time-tables and rail-roads; and when my train moved into the station, with alacrity I obeyed the summons, "All aboard!"

THE BEAVER RIVER WATERS.

CHAPTER XIII.

It was the May Term of Court. There was a lull in the proceedings, and the Judge slightly beckoning, I approached the bench.

"When are you going to the woods?" said he, unbending the awful brow of Justice, and with just the least unjudicial twinkle in his eye.

"I am thinking of taking in the Spring fishing, this year, Judge, up in the Beaver River country."

"Is your party made up?"

"Well, the Editor of the Diurnal is going, for one. He was such a 'hail fellow well met' last year that I was bound to have him with me this year. And the Manager of the Daily Flag Staff is going, so as to keep up the equipoise. There's room for one more. A quartette is as essential in the woods as in an organ-loft."

"They're both good fellows," his Honor added.

"If you'll enlist in this company, Judge, as a high-private, I'll stipulate that you shall have a good time,— weather and trout permitting."

"I'll go!" said the Judge, after a moment's reflection;— "Clerk, call a jury in No. 43."

In due time the Term ended, the necessary preliminaries were completed, and one afternoon, late in May, found us four at Utica waiting for the five o'clock train on the Black River Rail-Road.

That road is associated in many minds with the opening scenes of the delightful vacation months. When the summer days come, and one has a fish-rod in his hands, then "Black River Rail-Road" is a phrase to conjure with. The brain of the happy sportsman, at the sound of these magic words, is filled with pictures of camp and stream and lake; for this road, for many miles, skirts the wilderness, and almost every station is the gateway to Paradise.

"Trenton!" shouts the brakeman; and the passenger drops his paper, eagerly gazes out of the window, vainly striving to gain a single glimpse of the romantic and picturesque Trenton Falls.

At "Prospect" he remembers that here he may leave the train and find his way to Jock's Lake, or West Canada Creek, or, still further away, to Piseco and Pleasant Lakes, where, in olden times there has been untold sport.

At "Alder Creek" he is reminded of Woodhull, the Bisby Lakes, and Canachagala, with the famous Canachagala "spring-hole" beyond.

Then come "Booneville" and "Port Leyden," both entrances to the Moose River waters,—the Fulton Chain with its eight glittering lakes; the Brown Tract Inlet and the noble Raquette Lake beyond, easily accessible.

The traveler reaches "Martinsburgh" and "Lowville;" and "No. 4," the Beaver River Country, with the Tupper Lakes beyond, will inevitably come to mind, for these stations are the points of entrance to those localities.

And by connecting rail-roads one may, indeed, sweep northward, eastward and southward again, pretty much around the entire Adirondacks; and almost every station is "the best place," if we have faith in the local opinion, at which to enter the wilderness.

I trust, then, that the ties of that road may never decay, and its rails never wear out, and that it may always pay good dividends, for it is, *par excellence*, the highway to the gates of the Sportsman's Paradise.

The bags and bundles were, at length, all on board our train, our rods and guns carefully set up in the corners we appropriated without protest,—for again was the fishing rod a passport,—and we were hurried away, after a moderate fashion, northward. At Martinsburgh, Lewis met us and transported us to his hotel at Beach's Bridge. We were actually again on the way to the woods, and it was with ill-concealed impatience that we spent the hour of daylight that remained. A proposition to go up a little stream, in the evening, to catch suckers in a net, was half-complacently entertained, but our finer sportsman's instincts prevailed, and we went to bed instead.

With the early morning we were off for Fenton's—"No. 4,"—sixteen miles distant. Five miles from Fenton's we struck solid forest, our fair road disappeared, and there was tramping to be done. The guns were brought into requisition, and a pigeon stew for dinner fell to our aim. We arrived at Fenton's a little before noon.

"No. 4" is simply the number of the township; but that name abides although "men may come and men may go," and new landlords preside at the hotel long known as "Fenton's."

There is a large clearing, of several hundred acres, on the south side of Beaver Lake, now rapidly returning, for the most part, to a state of nature, where a little group of families find a home and employment in a shabby sort of farming, but principally in hunting, trapping and acting as guides. Old Chauncey Smith, the famous hunter of the region, now nearly eighty years of age, lives here, still feebly following his vocation, but happiest when describing the scenes and relating the exploits of his past life.

Fenton himself is a famous hunter, and is, in his way and place, a notable and superior man. Those who have made his house their home, for weeks and months, come to entertain feelings of warm friendship toward him. It is fortunate, indeed, that in so many instances, the proprietors of these forest hostelries are men of character and genuine refinement beneath the homespun garb and plain exterior. This fact makes it doubly agreeable and wholly feasible for entire families to enjoy, together, in the wilderness, a summer vacation which brings health and vigor and a knowledge of nature that mingles well with high attainments and culture and "exalted privileges" during the remainder of the year.

From Fenton's hotel, you look off to the north, down upon Beaver Lake, and across upon heavy forests climbing up the hills that help to form the basin within which the lake lies embowered. A walk of a few moments down the easy path brings you to the lake itself, where boats await the use of all guests.

Beaver River enters the lake by a succession of rapids and falls, which extend by a winding way a dozen miles up to Wardwell's, (now Dunbar's,) or Still-water. It leaves the lake in rapids again, and plunges over picturesque falls, to which the guests of the house make excursions with never-failing interest and delight.

At such a resort, the trout are always hunted and chased like a fleeing criminal, but they learn by experience great wisdom and discretion and teach it to their children; so that, pursued as they are, they maintain an existence in fair numbers, and, to a reasonable degree, reward the skillful fisherman. However, they seldom leap through the air, straight at the successful sportsman, like Murray's ferocious trout, nor attempt that other expedient of whirling 'round and 'round the boat in a contracting circle, in an effort to twist the fisherman's head off, as Warner felicitously and veraciously relates.

We enjoyed an afternoon's excursion down the lake to the outlet. The water was high and swift, and the Editor had an adventure—his boat striking upon a hidden rock—which for a half minute looked entirely unpropitious. It is his luck, however, to always get out of a difficulty in some way, and he still lives,—like the gentleman of color who remarked, with the wisdom of experience weighting every word, that he always noticed that if he lived by the fourth of July, he lived all the rest of the year!

We also, that evening, engaged four guides, procured supplies, and supplemented our outfit for our projected trip to and camping at Smith's Lake, forty-eight miles further into the wilderness. In the reprehensible drawing of lots for guides (the "reprehensible" being in the result) I drew John, "the Talker." But I forecast my calamity. I was then in blissful ignorance of what fate had awarded me, and will not now anticipate.

At four o'clock in the morning, we were up and away, on foot, followed by a team of horses conveying our baggage,—on our way through the forest, over a horrid road to "Still-water," or Wardwell's, eleven miles distant. One ordinarily likes better to read of the glories of an early, summer morning, than to actually get up and learn of its exalted beauty experimentally. But if there is ever an unfeigned joy, it is when one "going in," at the beginning of his vacation, sets out upon a walk through the genuine, unqualified forest, on such a bright, fresh, dewy morning as was vouchsafed to us. If Fenton's boarders had been awake, they would have witnessed certain caperings and saltations, on the part of our dignified company, during the brief delay before we finally set out, that would have entirely convinced them that something besides the wine of the air had been imbibed. Men off in the woods are, after all, only boys, of a larger growth, let out of school.

We took lunch in our pockets, not waiting for breakfast, and after an hour or two, finding a mossy bank by a little stream that had wandered but a few steps from the spring where it was born, we spread ourselves around, in a free-and-easy and miscellaneous way, and restored the waning freshness of our spirits with hard boiled eggs, sandwiches, and cold water. Then on again we went, up hill and down, skirting the mud-holes, crossing the small streams, after the usual fashion on a wild-woods road, until, at the end of four hours we reached Wardwell's.

The little log-house on the bluff looked out upon a bay, where the river rests before undertaking its rugged descent to Beaver Lake, while Twitchell creek comes in at the right, contributing the water of Twitchell Lake, famous for trout and deer. This seems to be an admirable point at which to stop, making it a base from which to go daily to many good fishing resorts. But it is "the last house," and few are content to remain here, while the lakes and streams beyond are so enticing. We had large and delicious trout for our combined breakfast and dinner, but to our queries as to where they came from, Wardwell's indefinite reply was, "Oh, we git 'em down in the basin,"—but he didn't. It is a point of honor with the keeper of that house, whoever he happens to be, never to tell the passer-by of the half dozen or so excellent fishing places, not an hour's walk distant; and he is a lucky fellow who learns of them, even if he remains there for days together.

Wardwell, himself, is a character, and a greater curiosity than anything he can exhibit to the tourist. He gets out his old rifle to show with what he has slain countless deer and knocked over now and then a "painter." But one of the sights is loose and is tied on with a leather string.

"Why don't you fix that sight, Wardwell?"

"Waal," in a long drawl, "I've been thinking on't, and some day when I git time I guess I'll have to go at it."

"Time? Don't you have time enough up here?"

"Waal, I guess I dew, but I don't git at it."

The roof of his little log-barn had tumbled in.

"What's the matter with your roof, Wardwell?"

"Waal, last winter the snow was oncommon heavy and broke it down."

"Why don't you repair it?" was asked, with a sly wink all around.

"Waal, I guess I'll have to git at it sometime—when I git time."

And so the imperturbable old man, driven to death in doing nothing, answered all the sly quizzing with a like response. Poor old fellow, his wife went crazy after that, and he removed down to Fenton's, where he will build a hotel if he ever "gits time." He is succeeded at Still-water by Dunbar, who is said to be a "square," live man.

There was a lively little philosophical discussion among us, who counted ourselves as pretty busy men at home, whether, on the whole, Wardwell's way of taking the worries and cares of life was not, after all that could be said to the contrary, about as wise as the opposite extreme. However, I think the enforced delay in our departure from his house gave the vastly preponderating majority of our party a bias against Wardwell's mode of doing business.

Beaver River, above Wardwell's to Albany Lake, is principally still-water. That usually means crookedness. When a river is not in a hurry, it wanders all about the country in a dazed, aimless way, as if it had lost sight of the principle of gravitation, and didn't know enough to run anywhere if there is no hill to run down. Beaver River, at any rate, seems to be greatly confused, seeking now this side, and then that, of the broad valley through which it winds, doubling back upon itself at almost every turn as if to see if the rest of the water was coming along all right. If there is one thing it fully understands, it is the principle of the loop, in all its possible variety. It makes more distance in a shorter direct advance than any other stream I know of. Of course, it takes a good deal of time for a river to do any business in this way; and it was unanimously voted that Beaver River was either the prógenitor of Wardwell, or that Wardwell was at least the god-father of the river. We never could quite settle that little question—we didn't "git time."

We slowly and surely wound our way up the river, crooked as it is, regardless of the fickle sun which shone now in our faces, next on our backs, and, again, impartially burning one ear and then the other—the worst intoxicated and most reckless sun that ever shone; or, was it dizzy from trying to watch the turns of Beaver River?

At five o'clock we were hungry again, and landed on a point of hard land, for supper. So were and did the bl..ck flies. We supposed when we left home that we were nicely and in a soldierly manner stealing a march on this enemy, and overwhelming him with the almanac. He was not due so early according to the entomological time-table, but he came, nevertheless—some millions of him. We disputed our coffee and hard-tack with him at "Black Fly Point"— a name born of our anguish—and then hastened on, eager to find a rest for the weary where the wicked fly would cease from troubling. The night was settling down upon us as we reached South Branch, and we pushed up that stream, a short distance, and made camp. While the guides were constructing a "bower of boughs" we cast our flies among the leaping trout, at the landing, and took a good number, but they were small.

As the darkness closed in upon us and we gathered before the rousing fire, and stretched our weary limbs upon our couch of fresh and fragrant hemlock boughs, we discovered, to our consternation, that the Manager and his guide were missing. They were uncontrovertibly lost or drowned, or both. What precise mishap had indeed befallen them in this inhospitable region we tried to imagine, but none of the theories of their absence satisfied the whole party,— doubtless because each man clung with affection and respect to his own view of the case. It was certain that our lost friend was without axe, blanket or camp-kit, although it was an equally certain and miserable fact that the entire food-supply of the party was with the missing boat, wherever that might be. The conclusive statement of our chief guide, upon this point, brought a groan from somewhere near the stomach of the Editor, while the Judge decided sententiously, quoting a semi-legal maxim in the body of his opinion, that "what can't be cured must be endured." The Thin Man, who had been gratifyingly successful with his rod, generously and (they said) rather patronizingly declared that there need be no fears for breakfast if all hands would be content to eat his trout.

CHAPTER XIV.

At length, however, our faith in the proverbial good sense of the Manager—to say nothing of our belief in Jove's care of wandering beggars—gradually dispelled our anxieties; we smoked and smoked, and slept. But our slumbers were not undisturbed. The owl saw our watch-fire and told other owls, and such an alarming chorus of inquiries followed as to "Who? Who? Who-o-o?" we were, that one reckless person, startled from sleep, responded in a very improper manner, "None of your —— business!" It was the general sentiment of the party, although, as we raised on our elbows, wide awake, we did not all endorse the emphasis of the phraseology in which it was uttered.

We settled down to sleep again, resolved to make a business of it, whoever might question our identity or our right to be there. The fire burned low, and the heavy breathing of tired men in slumber and the occasional snapping of the fire, were all the sounds that broke the deep stillness of the night in the forest. Suddenly a voice broke out, "Snakes! I felt a snake run across me!"

"Take your boots off," responded an angry sleeper, whose nap was thus rudely broken—"take your boots off, and you won't feel any snakes."

"Don't insinuate anything of that sort, my dear fellow,—it's snakes in dead earnest this time."

The Chief Guide now came to the front,—"Gentlemen, it's rabbits! They're thicker in these woods than toads after a shower. They always skip and scoot around camp after dark, looking for something to eat. I felt one nibbling at the toe of my boot, but scar't him off and went to sleep again.—There!"—going to the pile of luggage at the foot of a tree near by—"the pesky rascals have been gnawing my pack-straps! They'll gnaw greasy leather every time. I sha'n't go to sleep again to-night,—I'll build up a rousing fire and watch the little scamps or we sha'n't have a whole thing left by morning." And the faithful fellow did as he said, while the vision of snakes faded out entirely; and we slept again and dreamed of armies and hosts of light-footed but predatory rabbits surrounding our camp and waiting to see the Chief Guide nod before proceeding to gnaw the flesh off from our bones.

Morning brought a solution of the mystery of the Manager's absence, and the doubt upon which we had in a primitive way gone to bed, in the person of the Manager's guide. Indeed, he was more anxious than we. We were the "lost." He knew where he was all the while, but was unable to say whether we were as fortunate as to our own situation. The Chief Guide and he were discoursing as we awoke. It turned out that the Manager and his man had missed South Branch entirely, and gone five miles further up-stream, to "Little Rapids," where there was a sorry prospect for the night; but fortunately two gentlemen were there encamped for the night, and to their bed and board—such as they had to offer—the wanderers were invited. All this the guide related to us as we rubbed our eyes after our first sleep in camp for the trip; and then, since breakfast was only possible to us at Little Rapids, we tumbled into our boats and proceeded thither as speedily as possible.

Hastily crossing the carry there, of only a quarter of a mile, we came upon the Manager, sitting on a log, in all the solitary grandeur of a martyr,—with blotched face and hands, a red handkerchief about his neck, with eyes suggestive of a night of highly-seasoned social festivity, and as solemn as an owl.

"How are you, anyway?"

"Glad to find you safe and sound!"

"Thought you were lost, or drowned!"

"Might as well have been," replied the Manager to our varied salutations:—"I didn't sleep a wink, and I was cold,—and as soon as the sun was up this morning the black flies pounced on me as if it was their last chance. See my face?—and my hands? I'm about eaten up.—Oh, you may think it's fun to get lost, without a blanket, and sleep in perdition and wake up in———"

"Torment, I suspect you mean," politely suggested the Judge; "still, you come out pretty well, considering what might have happened."

"Trust a newspaper man to strike on his feet every time!" triumphantly added the Editor, who, however, had been slightly angry, the night before, at the intimation that his "snakes" were hypothetical.

Our breakfast was speedily got ready and set before us. The Manager had not in the least exaggerated the facts as to the black fly. The eating on our part, hungry as we were, was moderation to abstemiousness compared with the devouring which we suffered, in the hot sun, from myriads of the little black imps. We were almost driven to madness by their attacks, and were only too glad to push on up the river, as soon as possible, out of the reach of the fierce swarms, that seemed to stand guard on this vantage ground and challenge all invaders of the sacred solitudes beyond.

Proceeding up the river, we soon reached the foot of "Albany Carry," three-fourths of a mile long. Carries are all pretty much alike in that the guides must bear their inverted boats over their heads; and the sportsman, if he be a genuine one and physically capable of it, must bend his back to a load of luggage that out of the woods would make him shudder; and there is up hill and down, mud-holes and roots and prostrate trees and a vast deal of perspiration and fatigue. In the real wilderness there is no royal road over the carry. In this instance we were loaded with the heavy blankets necessary for the cool nights, and our food-supply and camp-kit, to say nothing of the useless articles one always brings to the woods; and doing our best, the guides were compelled to "double the carry" before we were ready to embark again.

A pleasant row of two or three miles, over what must be good fishing grounds in early spring, brought us to Albany Lake. This lake has shores which are attractive feeding grounds for deer. Passing through this body of water we entered and ascended the inlet to the rapids where another carry of three-fourths of a mile awaited us.

I have attainments useful and ornamental, but on this occasion, under the inspiration of hunger, I developed a talent for cookery, latent until then, which promises to serve me as good a turn in adversity as the trade which in some parts of the old world every son of fortune is compelled to learn. I dressed and broiled a trout on a twig, before an open fire, in a manner which, the Editor said, deserved a Special Notice—although the paragrapher would require a sample to be laid upon his table. The true editorial instinct, however, led him to remark, in quite an opposite spirit, as the last vestige of the broiled fish disappeared in the cook's mouth, that it was always your thin men who eat the most, and that Oliver Twist's cry for "more" was expressive of their constant state of stomach. The judicial mind, however, ruled that strict right wronged no man, and that a thin man, under the present constitution, and the amendments thereto, could not be coerced into surrendering any portion of his goods—without an equivalent, and then only by virtue of the right of eminent domain. He was pleased to add, also, to the gratification of all but the Editor, that dead-heading, in the wilderness *at least*, (with significant emphasis on the qualifying phrase) was not to be countenanced, and if any person (and he looked hard at the Editor) desired to eat the fruits of another person's skill, without his free consent, it was simply an indication that the distiction of *meum* and *tuum* was not duly regarded in that person's mind;—but at this instant the gravity of the Judge broke down, and we all joined in the laugh which the Editor caused by his successful personation of the culprit receiving sentence.

By this time we were all ready for the noon-day tramp over the carry. At the dam, in the swift water, there was very lively sport with the fly, among the small trout. The large ones had retired from the rapids, and the small ones had taken their places, as is likely to occur near the end of the time for fishing in swift water.

A short row (about two miles) up the river brought us to Smith's Lake—as pretty a sheet of water, with its seven wooded islands and charming, mountain-girt shores, as one is likely to see in the Adirondack region,—much like, indeed, but larger than Blue Mountain Lake, which is confessedly of surpassing beauty.

We took possession, by the sportsman's right, of the "Syracuse Camp," which its proprietors were to occupy later in the season.

The open sleeping camp was hardly tenantable, and we were glad to avail ourselves of a trapper's winter-hut of logs and bark, of entirely nondescript architectural design, but which contained a pile of stones for a fire-place, and a bed of marsh hay. We built a rousing fire, and a conflagration seemed imminent as the flames and smoke and sparks flew up the sheets of spruce bark that formed the side of the hut by the fire. But a trapper had, all alone, braved the rigors of the winter there, and doubtless had piled on the wood as freely in January as we needed to in May. At all events, the "fire risk" proved to be a good one, and despite our fears we learned to be comfortable on that score. A heavy rain that night searched out sundry defects in the roof, which were cured with fresh sheets of bark, the next day.

CHAPTER XV.

When the sun came up, fresh and vigorous, the next morning, flocks of cross-bills, more numerous than the sparrows in our eastern cities, fluttered and darted about our camp. The whir of their swift wings, and the clutch of their tiny claws on our bark-roof, woke us up. They were very inquisitive and fearless, and became great pets with us; although, each morning, somebody was disposed to anathematize them for disturbing our morning slumbers. They are such bright, cheerful and sociable little fellows,—chippering their quick, sharp notes through their cross twisted bills,—that I have become very fond of them, in these excursions in the wilderness, and have come to feel that they are an essential part of the accompaniments of a well regulated camp.

After breakfast we began to look about our surroundings and make our plans for the day. The "Syracuse Party," whose hospitalities, so far as shelter was concerned, we were enjoying, had an eye to the picturesque in selecting their camping ground. In the midst of the sloping clearing of two or three acres,—made to avoid falling trees and to escape the mosquitoes whose delight is damp and shady places among trees and shrubs,—they had erected the two or three bark structures which were open to all, or, as the spruce-bark sign read,

" All sportsmen welcome to its use.
But not abuse."

On the eastward, was a delightful view,—the semi-mountainous shores across the lake heavily wooded; while here and there the pretty, wooded islands looked like gems in their setting. At the left, rises Pratt's Mountain, or Smith's Rock,—the latter name sometimes bestowed in remembrance of a hermit who many years ago dwelt at its foot, cleared a few acres, and finally disappeared as mysteriously as he came. The lake also takes from him its name—not very distinctive among men, to be sure, but emphatically so among bodies of water where Round Pond, Clear Pond, Rock Pond, Bog Pond, and the like, occur with confusing reiteration.

We entered upon the enjoyment of our sojourn at this delightful place with great zeal. Rods and reels were speedily rigged and we set forth upon a tour of combined fishing and exploring. It had dawned upon us, as we were ascending the river, that the water was high, and we soon made the disagreeable discovery that it was too high for good fishing. We were late for the fishing on the rapids, and too early for the fishing at the spring-holes. The trout were in the unsettled state in which they always are, intermediate the times when they leave the rapids and gather at the spring-holes, and were wandering, at their own sweet will, all over the lake. We also found that for trout of any desirable size, we must troll along the shallows by the shores, where fair sized trout were hunting for minnows, or fish with bait off rocky points; and, saddest confession of all, the fly cast in the good orthodox way was almost useless anywhere except down the river upon the rapids. There one might have sport, such as it was, with the little fellows, and take trout in numbers to his satisfaction. The scales, however, brought mortification and regret. The wicked Herod himself would have shed tears to see what a heap of dead babies one afternoon's slaughter produced.

But a half loaf is better than none; and I maintain that a fisherman, who sulks in his tent,—like that graceless and obstinate hero, Achilles,—because he can't take trout with a fly while he can with bait, is, to say the least, more nice than wise. The most ardent fisherman whom it is my good fortune to know, the victor in many a contest of skill with the bamboo, the venerable and genial Reuben,—who fondles a favorite fly, frayed and ragged from the fight with a big trout, as a father fondles his first baby,—even Reuben, when he must do it, yields flies, leader, slender rod and all, and takes a "bait-pole." After him, let no common fisherman lift his nasal organ sky-ward and sniff, if fisherman's luck brings him to the woods at a time "between hay and grass," and only bait takes the fish.

Without describing the spirit in which we did it, it is sufficient to say that in this case we accepted the inevitable, and after a fair trial confined ourselves in the main to still bait fishing and trolling with the rod. It would afford me peculiar satisfaction, as a historian, to record triumphs such as the reader has only dreamed of; but for my own comfort and history's sake, I prefer to utter unpalatable truths rather than to indulge in the fictions of fancy. It was a solemn fact that we had made a mistake. We had studied the almanac but not the signs of the peculiar season. However, there was no sulky Achilles among us, and in the end we took the half loaf with philosophical cheerfulness.

After a forenoon of successful fishing, my guide "John" took me up the inlet. It is one of those dead, stagnant streams which one finds now and then slowly winding through a marsh. The alders and weeds were brown and dry, and everything was as cheerless and lonely as can be imagined. As we silently and slowly crept up the winding stream, watchful to detect the leap of the trout, the stillness was almost oppressive. There was no bird or animal life to break the spell of desolation, except the singular note of the bittern bearing the descriptive, popular name of "the pile-driver." The half dull, half-resonant "ca-thug! ca-thug!" of its voice was occasionally heard, and once the bird, startled by our unsuspected approach, sprang suddenly into the air, uttered a croaking "squawk" and flew heavily away. We lingered in this region of death and silence as long as I could endure it, and then hastened back to the sparkling waters of the lake, where our eyes could at least rest themselves on the green-clad islands and mountains, and our ears welcomed again the gurgle and murmur of the waters around the prow of our light and swift-moving boat.

This "John," who had fallen to my lot, was a singular character. He was absolutely lazy and useless about camp. Very likely he would have frozen and starved before he would have chopped wood for the night or prepared a breakfast. But he was as willing and free to row all day as the best of guides. The last thing at night, before going to bed, he would come to me and ask, "Don't you want to try the fishing before breakfast?"

"Don't care if I do, John; what time shall we start?"

"Five o'clock, or half-past, if you say so."

"All right, John. Call me, and I'm on hand."

At the appointed minute, in the morning, I would feel his touch and see his gesture; and creeping out of the hut as stealthily as he had entered it, without wakening a man, I followed him to the shore. Once in the boat he became "The Talker." In a drawling, half audible tone he slowly talked on and on and on, all day long, of his hunting and trapping and the wonderful affairs of which he had been a great part. His special theme, upon which he delighted to dwell at all times, was his "pardner," the hunter whose hut we were occupying. It did no good to interrupt him, or to request him to be silent. He was sure to find occasion and excuse for renewing his everlasting drawl in a low tone. His good nature and kindness, however, totally disarmed my indignation; but many a time I stepped on shore, after two or three hours of this Talker's afflictive society, with a sense of relief. I learned wisdom from this experience, and a burnt child would no sooner put his hand on a red-hot stove than I would again knowingly engage a "Talkative Guide."

We had varied success in fishing. My record one day was as follows: one trout before breakfast; from breakfast to dinner, three, one of them thirteen and a quarter inches long and seven and a half inches around; after dinner, by trolling with spoon, one salmon trout, fifteen inches long. The following day I took twenty six-trout, the largest being a half pound in weight. A day later I took, trolling with rod, two before breakfast; after breakfast and before dinner, nine, the largest, fourteen and a half inches long and seven inches around; after dinner, one. This was about the average fortune of the party.

The Editor was having excellent luck, one day, fishing from a rock opposite camp, when suddenly the trout ceased biting, and he began to take bull-heads. Determined to remove these invaders, he continued fishing until he had caught an amazing quantity, when they also suddenly disappeared, and sun-fish in great numbers appeared. The Editor finally abandoned the contest and left the "punkin seeds" in possession of the field.

The Judge was, at another time, the sole occupant of a shelving rock at a favorite point, and was fly-fishing with great zeal. We who were at a distance had our attention called to him by a capering and cavorting on the rock, that indicated great judicial excitement and, doubtless, a contest with a magnificent *salmo fontinalis*. Drawing near in our boats to witness the expected victory, we saw that by some ill-luck the fisherman's rod was broken, but he, thus disabled, was gallantly playing a fine trout up and down the water in front. Finally, by a magnificent run backwards—a victorious retreat—he landed his panting victim on the rock. It was a fine triumph of mind over matter, and we heartily cheered, while the Judge waved his broken rod and tangled line, and joined in the shouts.

On the northerly side of the lake, near Smith's clearing, is the outlet of Harrington's Pond, a goodly stream that comes tumbling down the rocks and forms a favorite pool for trout. We had some of our finest sport there, in water then about eight feet deep. There were also points in the lake where submerged islands just lifted their rocky crowns above the surface. These seemed to be chosen haunts of the trout, and we took our largest at such places. There are various small lakes and ponds, not distant and easily accessible, but we visited none of them. Later in the season they are said to afford rare sport.

CHAPTER XVI.

We had all the the enjoyment that a life in camp on the shores of a beautiful lake gives, day after day, but nothing occurred very notable to record. The evening camp-fire nightly brought us all together, and there was "fun alive." It was a favorite pastime of the Editor's, as bed-time approached, to relate "hair-lifting" stories of panthers and other wild animals that are supposed to lurk in the forest, but which no summer visitor ever sees. On one evening in particular he exerted his fancy to the utmost, but with such a truthful air that even the very elect would have been deceived, if they had not known the editorial capabilities in the way of invention. The forest seemed alive with tragedies ready to burst upon us from the black depths around. None of us would have been surprised if a pack of wolves had dashed down upon us across the clearing. A panther's scream in the darkness of the adjacent wilderness would have been as natural to the occasion as the darting flight of the cross-bills at sunrise. As we crawled into camp and went to bed, one, whose fortune it was to sleep at the end of the row, near the entrance over which hung a piece of bagging, displayed an unusual nervousness. Such is the inhumanity of man to man, that the rest also became very nervous, and expressed fears that as the fire burned low we might be attacked by some wild beast.

"Don't you suppose this door can be fastened, boys?" said the end man.

"Oh, no," responded a fortunate middle-man; "and a panther wouldn't mind that old rag, anyway, for a minute."

"We are lucky," said another insider, "if he don't pounce on this old bark roof, and come at us in that way."

"Hark!" cried, the man of nerves, "did you hear that?"

It was a piercing cry in the forest.

"What shall we do?" in chorus.

"Do?" answered the Editor, "say your prayers and go to sleep. It has come to a pretty pass, that a screech owl can drive you fellows all wild with fear."

The suppressed merriment exploded at this point, and the end man, sadly silent, laid himself down to sleep, wiser in wood-lore than he had been before. The Editor had his revenge for "snakes in his boots," but nobody was afraid of panthers after that.

The days go on in the wilderness all too swiftly. To the lover of the woods no hours drag heavily, except when a long, drizzling rain settles down over forest and lake, and there are only the camp and the smudge and the old worn-out stories to entertain. It must be confessed that when such hours drag out into days they are severely irksome, and one thinks of comfortable office and home library and domestic circle. But when the sun comes out again, the transformation both of nature and the camper's spirits is complete. Then the life of the woods seems doubly joyous. The day of departure is no longer looked for with yearning but with dread and impatience. A single day of storm and drizzle is wretched enough, but the succeeding days are doubly delightful for the enforced inactivity and discomfort.

Luckily we had no rainy days, although now and then a dashing shower, after the genuine Adirondack fashion, reminded us that nature held in her urn all sorts of gifts.

But every camping experience has its final day. The baggage is repacked, the tent pins pulled, the rods unjointed, the last things picked up, and all stowed away in the marvelous boats of those forest lakes and streams, and faces are turned home-ward. Our time was up one day in June. The Judge was to hold Court somewhere on a certain day We broke camp early in the morning and set out for home. In passing through Albany Lake we encountered a terrific thunderstorm with high wind. Our frail boats were tossed and driven and rocked in a most uncomfortable way for fifteen minutes, and then the wind lulled, the storm passed away, and the sun shone out with an innocent surprise as if to ask what the elements had been doing while he stepped behind a cloud for a few minutes to make his before-dinner toilet.

My guide, in a little spurt of speed, racing with another boat in Albany Lake, broke an oar, we went ashore at the first opportunity, changed seats, and he paddled the thirty miles to Wardwell's. That took a good deal of the talk out of him, and I enjoyed his society more than I had done at any time before. We took dinner at Little Rapids, where the Manager on the upward trip spent his eventful night with the mosquitoes, and his morning with the black flies. The Manager's blood was evidently bad—for most of the flies were dead and gone!

While dinner was preparing, I clambered out upon the rocks in the rapids—hungry to the last for a little more fly-casting—and took several gamy little fellows in the eddies and pools behind the rocks. Then I unjointed my rod for good and all.

On the way down the crooked river again we encountered another terrific thunderstorm. It may have been the same one that attacked us so fiercely in Albany Lake, and which, in descending the river, got all tangled up, lost the points of compass and unwittingly took the back-track. It had, however, lost much of it vigor, although where it got all the water that poured down is still a marvel. We endured it—man and guide—as long as we could, bailing the boat occasionally, until it seemed good to us to "let it rain" while we went ashore for shelter. An Adirondack boatman always carries his shelter with him—his boat. We drew ours ashore, turned it over, crept under, and were safe from the pelting of the storm.

At five P. M. we were at Wardwell's again. We had had enough work for one day, and remained here over night. The next morning we walked the eleven miles to Fenton's, in four hours; breathed, repacked, dined and dressed for civilization; walked five miles further, out of the woods, and then took seats in the wagon conveying our luggage; bent our heads to the third thunder-shower of the day; and reached Lowville in time for supper and the 6:23 P. M. train, which we took for Utica and beyond.

Once on a railway train, homeward bound, woodsmen are no better, not much wiser, no happier—yes, happier!—than other people.

Through the Wilderness,

FROM

Booneville to Saratoga.

CHAPTER XVII.

The following correspondence explains itself:—

(1.)

DEAR MR. GRAVES:

I want a guide for two. Mr. Wallace (of the Guide Book) tells me you are a genuine sportsman yourself, and a good friend of sportsmen,—that I may write to you freely for information, and that you will as freely give.

I am going across the wilderness by way of the Fulton Chain, Raquette Lake, and so on,—time, two or three weeks,—right after July 4th, if my clients will let me. I am to take with me my son, a lad of eleven years—we two, no more. I shall come with all needed supplies and some pet notions of mine by way of tent and camping-kit. My boy is a strong, healthy, plucky little fellow, and I shall have no fears that he will give out where I don't.

My guide must be a careful, discreet, judicious man, and a good woodsman,—not profane, not foul-mouthed, not too talkative, temperate.

Have you in mind such a man as I want?

Yours Truly,
———.

(2.)

Boonerille, N. Y., June, 1877.

DEAR SIR :—

I have just the man you want—John L. Brinckerhoof, a middle-aged man of character in this town—the best guide in the woods. I have seen him and read him your letter. He says he will go with you. His terms, with boat, are $3.00 a day. I can get you a man for $2.50, but John is worth half a dollar a day more than any body else I know of. Write me if you want him.

Yours, B. P. GRAVES.

(3.)

Telegram.

B. P. *Graves, Booneville, N. Y.:*—

Engage Brinckerhoof. Will reach [...] train, July 5th.

I kept my telegraphed promise. [...] early morning, a bright-faced, en[...] youngerly gentleman stepped up t[...] moment on the platform, and said, "[...] I assured him that was my name. It w[...] addressed me. He convoyed my so[...] to the hotel, ordered our luggage sent [...] sion of us as one likes to be posses[...] ahead friend who knows better than y[...] done.

While we were waiting for bre[...] robust young men came into the ho[...] out to me as guides. I fell into c[...] and found them such honest, sens[...] lows, that I half repented having al[...] ment. "John" came in, soon a[...] known to me. He seemed to be a [...]

age; was large, compact and strong; had a face which nature intended for that of a general, and as honest as the sun, and a quiet, self-respectful, sensible way of talking which won my heart from the first. "Graves is right," thought I; "this is just the man for me,—he's got a head, as well as a good body and strong arms." And I never had occasion to change my opinion.

Phelps provided a pair of horses, wagon and driver; and after a substantial breakfast we set out on our way to "Old Forge" at the foot of the Fulton Chain of lakes, twenty-six and a half miles distant. To Moose River village, or Lawrence's, twelve and a half miles,—a little settlement in the woods clustered about the large tannery there established—the road was quite fair. Here we dined, and after an hour or more resumed our journey, but in quite a different manner. We left our wagon,—for it was useless beyond this point; our horses were made to swim across Moose River, which is here quite a broad stream; we were ferried over, and on the further shore we prepared for the serious and hard work of the trip. All our luggage, except rods and rifles, was piled, packed and strapped on the back of one horse, while the other was saddled for Ned and myself to ride alternately.

And while we are lying on the grass, in the shade of a wild cherry tree, and the driver and John are carefully arranging the load on the pack-horse, I am sure it will be of interest to the practical sportsman if I describe in detail what we took to the woods:

First.—A rubber "navy-bag," containing extra clothes

for two; tin pail which contained cooking and table outfit for four; small hand-bag, containing fly-book well furnished, lines, reels and many minor articles, and all the little odds and ends of things which experience had taught me are so convenient in camp,—all in the navy-bag, snug and dry.

Second.—Bundle, or pack,—made up of a light camp-stove, constructed from a plan of my own, (folding up much like an envelope); a cotton "A" tent, water-proofed and weighing ten pounds; heavy blankets; small, short-handled axe in sheath; landing-net with short handle,—all wrapped and strapped inside of a large piece of enameled cloth to be used to spread upon our bed of boughs, in place of rubber blanket.

Third.—Box containing provisions, weighing sixty-five pounds,—the box fitted with trunk straps with shoulder loops for carrying as a pack.

Fourth.—Loose articles,—fish-basket filled with "sundries;" two fly-rods and one bait-rod, firmly strapped together; two light, summer overcoats, and two rubber overcoats; and a Stevens' "Hunters' Pet" rifle in a leather case.

The entire luggage above mentioned—being house, stove, cooking and table utensils, provisions (with minor omissions) for three persons for two weeks, sporting outfit, etc., etc., weighed one hundred and sixty-five pounds, not guessed, but by Fairbanks' scales. I add with some pride but entire sincerity that this outfit proved to be admirable and complete beyond expectation; and, with added experience, I can think of nothing more that I would provide for a similar trip.

But the packing is completed, it is nearly two o'clock, and we have fourteen miles through the woods to accomplish, before night, over a notably rough road; and John has given the word, "all ready!" Our driver leads the way, driving the pack-horse before him without rein, leaving him to pick the path which his sagacity and experience helps him to do better than a man could do it for him; Ned is perched on the saddle horse and follows; I shoulder the bundle of rods and keep at the horse's heels; while John brings up the rear with the "Hunters' Pet" in his hand.

Nothing good could be said of the road, and nothing worse than that it was after the fashion of wilderness roads. It was through a dense forest, a mere wagon track full of mud-holes, with rocks, roots, hills, and corduroy bridges. The passage is sometimes made, at the driest season, with the "buck-board" wagon, but horse-back riding or walking is preferable. Ladies have passed over the road—American ladies at that—but they do not go at the break-neck speed that we went. We made the fourteen miles in four hours and twenty minutes; and fresh from my office, I managed, without detriment or great fatigue, to walk ten miles of the fourteen.

Before reaching Old Forge, and two miles distant, we passed the old "Arnold Place," famous in its day as the favorite resort of sportsmen of the old school, but now gone to decay and utterly abandoned. It is, indeed, the last house of the little settlement commenced by Herreshoff, son-in-law of John Brown of Providence, Rhode Island, after whom "John Brown's Tract" is named. Brown, in 1793, purchased 210,000 acres of the wild lands lying about the head-waters of Moose River. Herreshoff cleared about 2000 acres, erected many buildings, gathered there thirty or forty families, built a dam and constructed a forge, undertook the manufacture of iron, which effort proved a costly failure—and blew his brains out. The wilderness is now claiming its own and slowly creeping in upon the two thousand acres once torn from it. The last house is in ruins, itself the scene of a brutal murder; and only the familiar swallows hovering about the deserted barns, or skimming over the grass-grown fields, with happy twitter, in the bright sunshine, pleasantly remind the passer-by of the life and activity and homes once existing there.

It was a delightful change of scene that met our eyes as we let down the bars and passed through the garden enclosure back of "Old Forge Hotel," a little way down the river below First Lake. As our modest cavalcade wheeled around in front of the hotel, the "old, old" smudge met our gaze, a party of Rochester sportsmen nodded pleasantly to us from the rude verandah, the small boy of the place, with hands in his pockets, approached and stared at Ned as being an unaccustomed visitor and a congenial spirit, and at length our host, Comstock himself, emerged from the kitchen where supper was brewing, and greeted his newly arrived guests. The splint-bottomed arm-chairs on the verandah invited us to rest, and we sank into them with the accumulated emphasis of our fourteen miles of pedestrian and equine travel added to wagon and rail-road ride and superlatively early rising at Utica after a very late retiring and previous journeying.

But we were not too hungry nor too weary to observe what a, quiet, charming out-look there was. Down the grass-plot, easterly a few rods, gleamed the Moose River waters, deep and sluggish, retarded in their flow by the dam at our left. The forest in this direction had hardly been broken. In the distance the mountains lifted their heads in the light of the descending sun. Within us was the feeling that the inevitably hard and tiresome "going in" had been accomplished, and that now and here really began the unalloyed delights Ned and I had talked over so often--both with boyish enthusiasm—at the winter fireside, and more frequently out under the trees on the lawn where the boys had pitched the tent, when the summer heats had begun to glow and the pavements were hot, and the air of office and school-room was stifling.

At supper two brown, blue-shirted young men sat at the table on my left. I thought they were guides, who by the *genius loci* had been, according to the fashion of the woods, invited to the "first table." Some common enough Latin phrase uttered in joke between them, however, attracted my attention, and I speedily learned that my two table neighbors were students from Hamilton College. That being my own Alma Mater, I was quickly on good terms with them, and they related to me the history of their adventures thus far. Said one of them:

"We resolved, last winter, to do the woods this summer.

We built a boat, at odd times, studied up the maps and guide-books, and the question of out-fit and supplies, and got everything, route and all, down to a fine point. We shipped our boat by rail to Booneville, had it transported by wagon to Moose River Village, and, having been told that the river was navigable from that point up to the lakes, we put our boat into the water there. That was two days ago.

"The river is navigable after a fashion, to be sure, or we shouldn't be here now. But it is full of snags, rocks and rapids, and we made very slow progress and had a hard time of it. The night that we spent on the way, it rained fearfully. We carry for our bed, and swing between two trees, a double-length hammock and sleep in it, feet to feet. In place of a tent we have a rubber blanket long enough to cover us both completely, heads and all. That was the way we camped in the rain, the horrid din of a thunderstorm with fearfully vivid lightning all about us. For cooking utensils we have only a frying-pan."

"No coffee-pot?" inquired I in amazement.

"No; after we have fried our pork or trout, we scrub out the frying-pan and make coffee in it."

"Spare me, on that," I said; "I want my coffee in the woods as good as at my own breakfast table,—other cooking will take care of itself, with such appetite as the woods give."

"Oh, it does the business well enough, on a pinch; and we were bound to reduce our luggage to the lowest possible point. Why, knives and forks and a spoon or two, and tin cups, a lantern, axe, fishing tackle and rifle, complete our out-fit. I admit that we are "roughing it" in good earnest. At all events, the journey up here from Lawrence's deserves that appellation. But, '*forsan et haec olim meminisse juvabit*'—which, freely translated, means, 'it will make a good story to tell at college next winter.' However, I shall have to tone it down a little, or the boys won't believe it."

"They will doubtless," I said, "hurl back at you, '*possunt quia posse videntur*,' and translate it to suit themselves: 'Your big thing was all in the thinking.'"

"Oh, no; I don't fear that, if I can only preserve for future reference the scars of some of these big blisters."

When I saw the narrator of this story, as I did the following summer, bearing from the commencement stage his graduating honors and plentiful boquets, I was thinking, I confess, more of the woods and of our interview at Old Forge than of his strong and graceful oration and manly presence—and I had not forgotten the blisters.

It was nearly eight o'clock in the evening when John took our luggage on his broad, strong shoulders down to the boat-house where his own beautiful Adirondack boat—his special joy and pride—awaited us. A pleasant row up the river by the fading light, and in the cool evening air, was a blissful change from our hard journey through the woods on foot and horse-back. We passed "Murderer's Point," where Nat Foster shot the Indian, Drid, as he was rowing up the river. John told the story, but it is better told in H. Perry Smith's "Summerings in the Wilderness."

It was after nine o'clock when, after having crossed First Lake in the darkness, our boat grated upon the sands and our long day's travel was done. We had arrived at "Stickney Camp" situate near the end of a narrow ridge or long neck of land running out to a point from the north shore and forming the division between First and Second Lakes. The "Camp" consists of two well built, shingle-roofed log-houses, about twenty-five by twenty-eight feet, and one and a half stories high, a corner of each nearly touching a corner of the other, like the squares on a chess board. Ample verandahs run nearly around each building. One structure was closed to all except the immediate friends of the owner. The other was at the disposal of our guide, he having erected the buildings and having for years been the guide of the "Stickney Party." A framed building, used as a boat-house below and general depository above, stands on the shore of Second Lake, and an ice-house, well filled every season, burrows under the protecting shade of some thickly growing trees. The under-brush is cut away, leaving large pine and other trees which afford ample shade but permit the black flies, "punkies" and mosquitoes little refuge from the breeze that almost continually blows from one lake or the other.

The house we occupied had a well appointed and furnished kitchen, as to essentials. Its rude walls were lined with fishing tackle, tools to mend a gun, a rod or a boat with, and no limit of convenient odds and ends of woodsy things, affording abundant entertainment and study on a rainy day, and exceedingly handy in case of almost any conceivable break-down. The cup-board would have done credit to a good, motherly house-wife. The dining-room was ample and contained a table at which twenty hungry men might sit at ease while John should load it down with the marvelous results of his delicious forest cookery. Through the open doors and windows of the dining-room one could look upon the waters of two lakes, and hear the wavelets "*lap, lap*" on either shore. Above were two well lighted and comfortable sleeping rooms, one for guides and the other for "the party,"—the latter room furnished with beds having springs, mattresses, sheets and mosquito bars, —things not orthodox in the woods, to be sure, but amazingly comfortable.

We did not learn all this upon the night of our arrival, for we speedily found our way to our good beds and slept the glorious sleep of the woods. "Stickney Camp," of blessed memory, was our delightful home for several days, every waking hour of which was one prolonged dream of peace and rest and beauty. The lullaby of the waves and the tender sighing of the pines at our chamber window made two or three nights memorable as occasions when one was soothed so sweetly to slumber, and yet so gently moved to pleasant thoughts, that it seemed ungrateful not to yield to the soothing and also a cruel loss not to drink the inspiration of the hour and the sweet sounds to the full. Lying on the pine-leaf-sprinkled knolls in the shade, and looking off upon the glancing and glistering waters gently moved by the breeze under the bright sun, and feeling the resinous breath of the cool forest on the cheek, was rest to heart and mind as well as health to nerve and delight to the eye; and the sense of beauty grew like an infant drawing new life from the maternal fount. John, tireless, faithful, kind, to-be-depended-on, unobtrusive, busy about the household duties, added to rather than detracted from this sense of delicious peace and rest and enjoyment of nature. No other vacation scene of camp, or voyage, or glorious sport with rod and reel, ever comes back to memory so frequently or with such perfect and entire satisfaction, refreshment and delight as this at "Stickney Camp."

I saw, too, all these things through the fresh, young eyes of a boy of vigorous mind and body. I shared his healthy and entirely natural sensations. And I suppose the father's heart was gladdened by the happiness of his first born.

CHAPTER XVIII.

On the morning of our first day in camp, the college boys called upon us on their way up the Fulton Chain, and on to the St. Lawrence by Raquette River. They had entirely recovered from their hard trip up Moose river to Old Forge, and entered with spirit upon the long and difficult journey that awaited them. We tried to induce them to tarry with us for a day, but they were eager to enjoy "the real thing"; and we parted with them most reluctantly.

A "good provider" was our John, and he believed in a well filled larder. If a garden could have been extemporized, I have no doubt we should have had all the summer vegetables at our door. The next best thing was to "bait the buoys," and then take from the lake—the forester's garden, granary and butcher-shop—a pair of salmon trout whenever desired for a change, or to eke out fisherman's luck in catching speckled trout. Indeed, as John broiled the former, only for the catching of them, I should have been content to leave the speckled trout to their own devices. Our very first fishing experience on the Fulton Chain, therefore, was in taking minnows. The lad was expert at that, and was delighted with the sprightly sport. These tiny, timid fish, found in the shallow water near the shores, when caught were cut in pieces and scattered in deep water about the anchored stone attached by a long rope to a floating stick or buoy. After a day or two, we baited our large, strong hooks with live minnows and angled for the salmon trout which had found these places good feeding grounds. They took the bait very gently and deliberately, a sudden pull fixed the steel in their strong jaws, and then such a commotion! Hand over hand we pulled them right up to the surface and flopped them into the boat without giving them an inch of line or an instant to meditate a counter movement. It was the only safe way to deal with them. There was a certain sort of sport in this fishing, but it was chiefly a matter of brute force and a good breakfast.

After baiting the buoys, and thus amply providing for our table wants thereafter, and with a soldier's wisdom protecting the line of a possible retreat, we opened the real fishing campaign at "the marsh." A cold stream winds its sluggish current through a swamp on the southeast side of First Lake, that years ago was and still is flooded by the dam at Old Forge. We cast our flies in the clear, deep pools, occurring here and there in the course of the stream, and surrounded by ghostly dead trees that still resist decay, and by graceful but troublesome lily-pads. The lad had never fished with the fly before, and after some minor disasters readily consented to take his first lessons in open water. In a few minutes I took fifteen trout, most of them small, and, these being all we wanted for dinner, we returned to camp. The remainder of the day was charming, out under the trees; and as we were content to take whatever of enjoyment the wilderness brought us, we lay on the ground in the shade, were fanned by the breeze that had arisen, looked out upon the waters and the grand old forests, and talked away the hours (the boy had no end of talk in him) until balmy night came again.

The next morning John brought in a two-pound salmon trout for breakfast. In the afternoon we went up through Second and Third, and into Fourth Lake about half its length, to Jack Shepperd's camp, situate in a grove of small spruces, on the south shore. Jack is one of the noted guides of the region, and he has a most comfortable sportsman's abiding-place. There were at that time five "camps"—substantial buildings—on Fourth Lake; Snyder Camp, Sam Dunakin's and Lawrence's on the north shore, and Shepperd's and Pratt's on the south shore, all private but Shepperd's and Dunakin's, which were for the entertainment of all who would pay for it.

On our return, just at sunset, we had some very pretty sport at the head of Fourth Lake outlet. Ned struck a half-pound trout, and with boyish impetuosity gave a tremendous jerk, and broke a second joint. The poor fellow's heart was almost as badly broken, thinking that his rod was ruined and his fun was all up for the trip. But that evening John, our good genius, mended and made it about as good as new. The lad afterwards, with a little instruction, acquired considerable skill with the fly-rod, and was sometimes elated with success superior to that of his elders. A boy may be trusted to pick up a knowledge of fishing and all the kinks and knacks, quite as readily as grown people. Indeed, I doubt whether any body can handle a pin-hook with such remarkable success as a boy does. I suppose this intuitive knowledge of "how to take fish" implies that our remote ancestors went a-fishing for a living for many generations, and that their then acquired skill and habits come out naturally in a boy before his nature is overlaid by the discipline and results of modern education.

The following day was Sunday. John announced that we had eaten up everything in the way of our fish-supply and suggested that there must be a pair of salmon trout at the buoy waiting for us. We went to our preserve. Making a virtuous necessity of it, in a few moments we took three salmon trout weighing two and a quarter, one and three-quarters, and one and a half pounds respectively, and a speckled trout weighing a half-pound. They made a breakfast befitting the day,—and it required something remarkable to befit such a day as that was, for it was perfection itself.

The weather has much to do with the enjoyment of people of in-door life, to be sure; but in the woods, when you are camping or tramping, it is the all-important thing. It makes or mars your out-door life. A fortnight of rain in the midst of your sojourn in the forest is a calamity without mitigation or compensation. But perfect weather among the trees and on the lakes and streams—that is blessedness itself.

In the afternoon we went to church on the summit of Bald Mountain, and worshipped Nature. We made the ascent from the north shore of Third Lake, by a good trail, and spent about two hours on the heights. We gathered wild strawberries out of the crevices of the rocks ; looked upon lakes and less lofty mountains as though they were spread out upon a map ; looked down into an ancient beaver-meadow in a valley on the north side of the mountain, through which a little stream was quietly wandering ; and inscribed our names on the timbers of Colvin's Signal Station. The southern face of the mountain is almost perpendicular rock, and its summit is nearly bald, whence its name. We gazed far to the westward, toward the region of church-spires and happy homes ; but, as far as the eye could reach and distinguish, the forest extended in hilly waves and billows. On the east, afar off, was Blue Mountain. Northward we dimly saw mountains which we could not distinguish ; and on every side, forest and lake and hill and mountain stretched away into the distance. But the most beautiful sight was below us—First, Second, Third and Fourth Lakes in the Fulton Chain—glittering links, indeed, as we saw them shining in the clear sunlight.

Nothing repays better in the woods than climbing mountains. The views from their summits are not only exceedingly grand and beautiful, but one also gains a comprehension of the vastness and the general features of the wilderness that nothing else can give.

If we had any doubts about the propriety of taking our breakfast out of the water in the soberest and least sportsman-like way, that Sunday morning, we had no misgivings whatever about our mountain church-going, when we returned that evening to camp, full of the influences gathered on the heights out of the heavens around us and from the beautiful forest beneath. And although more than two hundred years of ancestral Puritan blue blood and teachings flow in my veins and conscience, and the venerated past lifts a very conspicuous finger of warning as to any infringement of Sunday sanctities, I am bold to declare that I went to bed that night and slept without a troubled dream from Puritan ancestor or from any other source.

Monday, while John was doing up the morning's domestic work, the boy and I struck a bonanza in a pile of empty fruit-cans, left by some former occupants of our sylvan home. These we tossed into the water, and as they floated away before the breeze we practiced on them our skill in rifle-shooting. The "Running Deer" at Creedmoor may be all very well in its way, but give me, for a little exhilarating sport, rifle-shooting at empty tin-cans floating out from shore, dancing on the waves, and scudding before the wind. "A hit! a palpable hit!" is indeed palpable, for if you are a good marksman, your tin vessel sinks like an iron-clad, when it is bored through and through. The staid and "much-experienced" John was happy to take half a dozen shots with us, and enjoyed demolishing a tin-can with as much delight as Ned himself.

Then we went to "the marsh," where, with the fly, I took thirty-eight trout in about two hours. Of course, I lost my "biggest fish"—every body does; but any big fish knows how, in a small pool surrounded by lily-pads, to get most completely lost.

On Tuesday, starting at noon, we made an afternoon trip to Little Moose and Panther Lakes, which lie in the course of the South Branch of Moose River. The first named lake is surrounded by beautiful shores, and is a charming sheet of water. The day was too bright for good fishing, but we enjoyed rowing and exploring, and have pleasant recollections associated with the lake. Panther Lake, a wild, lonely little body of water, is a gem of exquisite beauty set in the green of the forest. Out of the traveled course of tourists and sportsmen, without a sign of human occupation, it is as purely a poet's dream of wildness and nature's own inner sanctuary as anything I ever saw.

The carries were only seventeen minutes from First Lake to Little Moose, and six minutes from that to Panther Lake. John thought nothing of "backing" his boat over them both, going and coming, and rowing on the lakes all we desired.

That evening an in-coming party halted at our camp and brought a letter,—the first and only one we received during our entire trip across the wilderness. A rolling stone gathers no moss,—and a roving fisherman gets few letters.

An early breakfast on the following day—and at 8:30 A. M. we were off on another excursion, to visit the North Branch of Moose River. We went through Second and Third Lakes of the Chain, and into Fourth to the carry near Snyder's Camp, on the north shore, where we crossed over to "Carry Pond," five-eighths of a mile. John backed his boat, while the lad and I carried the oars, rubber coats, lunch, rifle and fly-rods. Crossing the Pond,—

and frightening a flock of ducks on our way,—we made another carry of one mile to First Lake of North Branch. We continued up the lake and the river to the rapids, fishing at various spring-holes on our way. At the foot of the rapids we left the boat and went a little distance up the carry which leads to Second Lake. Beyond this is Big Moose Lake, a famous and favorite body of water for camp and sport.

We had no marked success in fishing, during the day, but on our return to camp we lingered, as the sun was descending, at the outlet of Fourth Lake where we always found trout waiting for our flies. We took our share, and went home satisfied with having made a very interesting expedition. I mention these little excursions in detail, in part to show how easily one in camp may visit many delightful resorts and break up the monotonous life one naturally falls into—however pleasant it may be—when settled down in one place. I greatly enjoy seeking out new lakes and streams in the woods. There is an infinite variety in them, after all, and they each have individual peculiarities which any ordinary observer can hardly fail to note, and which bring new delight to the lover of woods and waters.

CHAPTER XIX.

A little more of the serene and happy life at ("Stickney Camp," during which I had almost forgotten that I was to cross the wilderness, and the migratory impulse came upon me. Already I longed for the charms of Seventh Lake, and the glories of the Raquette, while Utowana, Eagle and Blue Mountain Lakes lured me in the distance. And the boy—he had never been quite content to sleep in John's comfortable quarters. Nothing short of tent and bed of boughs and out-of-door cookery, and lakes where there was no highway for parties coming and going, would wholly satisfy him. John, I was convinced, was conspiring with himself to make us so completely happy here that we would willingly surrender our projected journey further. He had "roughed it" enough, slept on beds of boughs in winter as well as in summer, until a mattress was good enough for him; and his kitchen stove was vastly more convenient than any open fire or any new-fangled affair that a sportsman might lug into the woods with him. On the one side, therefore, was the luxury of this present life at Stickney Camp, and John's unspoken but not unfelt persuasion to remain. On the other, was my programme, deliberately formed, which urged me on like another Wandering Jew, and Ned also, who teased and talked me wild when we went to bed and when we woke in the morning and during the day,—when John was absent,—all combining to make me shake off the lethargy of luxury and go forth to new fields and fortunes.

It was a delicate matter; but one day I unpacked my big bundle and brought forth to John's gaze the tent I had brought, and the camp-stove—flat as a pan-cake—that I had with much self-gratulation, invented and caused to be constructed; and then, diving down into the depths of the navy-bag, brought forth also the tin pail which contained a complete "kit" for stove and table. I spread them all out before him. John looked at them, and I looked at John, awaiting in silence his verdict. Of course it was my right to order my own coming and going, and his, too; but I loved John, and I wanted to please him, and did not want to drag an unwilling guide through the woods, whatever my rights were. He said not a word, but I saw that the hope he had cherished had gone out of his heart. I thought I perceived, also, a respectful and internal sniff at my pet and pride, the wonderful camp-stove. However, it was at length agreed that the next morning we should pack up and begin our wanderings.

It was half-past ten o'clock when John put the big key over the door and before we were finally off—we three, and our entire luggage consisting of house and home as well as food-supply and personal effects, all stowed snugly away in John's boat. It was like leaving home. And the good roof and comfortable beds, the verandah with its memories of evening chats, the shady pines and spruces and hemlocks, the knolls and grass-plots where we had lounged, the charming water and forest views, and even the chippery cross-bills that were as sociable and friendly as Adam's companions of the brute creation, were all so many cords to sever. The boy, however, severed them easily enough. He was the happy one of the party as we waved adieu to "Stickney Camp" and swept away over the waters with the strong, steady stroke of John's oars. My eyes have seen "Stickney Camp" no more; but my dreams by night and by day, have many, many times re-lived the delightful life we spent there; and I hope for one more summer rest there with John and with not one, but with three sturdy boys.

Stopping at Jack Shepperd's Camp a few minutes we replenished our stock of provisions with butter and Bermuda onions. I cannot sing the praises of this vegetable too loudly as a good thing to have in camp. It fills the place of a dozen other things in the *menu* of the wilderness. One, indeed, is entirely independent and may defy famine on a lonely tramp, or driven ashore by storm a dozen miles from camp, if he has one pocket full of crackers, and a half-dozen Bermuda onions stowed away in other pockets.

When we reached the head of Fourth Lake, (near which the attractive Pratt Camp is situated,) John pushed up the shallow and rapid inlet while Ned and I walked, only a short distance, to Fifth Lake where we again took the boat. This latter lake is a small and unattractive sheet of water, useful, mainly, as a link in the chain. From Fifth to Sixth Lake we made our first carry, three-quarters of a mile.

John carried a pack-basket filled with provisions, his boat, oars and axe—a good load for an ox. The lad carried the "batter-pail" (with its germinal possibilities of unlimited pan-cakes) and a goodly assortment of small articles; while I struggled along under a pack made up of a bundle containing stove, tent, blankets and the navy-bag full of clothing etc., etc., and rifle, rods, small bag, and pail containing our cooking utensils and table furniture,—in all nearly one hundred pounds. We thus carried everything at one trip, but it was too much for us, and we were wiser afterwards. I had never so fully realized with what force the heart can pump blood up through the arteries in the neck and temples. I have great respect for the power of the heart, in a literal sense. And I know why a locomotive puffs so fiercely at the head of a long freight train on an up-grade. It is on a carry with a full load.

Sixth Lake is small, also, and the passage from it to Seventh is difficult, but no carry is necessary. As we emerged from the narrow, crooked stream, the beautiful Seventh, bathed in the rays of the descending sun, greeted our glad vision, and we felt rewarded for all the toil of nearly four hours the sight had cost us. Without stopping to land or select our camping-ground, we rigged our rods, and began seeking our supper. Sentiment and sleep were to come afterwards. The emergent necessity was something to eat. A promising spring-hole near the outlet gave us nothing; but, at the mouth of a stream putting in from the south shore, nearly opposite the foot of Big Island, in an hour's time we captured not only our supper, but an abundant breakfast. This, indeed, during our stay at Seventh, was our favorite resort, and we never failed to have fine sport with the gamy trout that came up from the lake as fast as we caught out the belligerents already in occupation. There was abundant, open, clear water to play them in, and taking trout in such a place is, to my mind, the very luxury and perfection of fishing with the fly.

Supper doubly assured by our success with our rods, we sought a spot for our temporary home. We had all the lake shore before us, where to choose, but there is a world of wisdom in choosing the right place. First of all, there is good, cold spring water to be thought of; then shade and dry ground; wood for camp-fire; a place not productive of mosquitoes, and one, if possible with other conditions, where the breeze will blow them away as fast as they come; trees likely to blow down upon you are to be avoided; reasonable nearness to good fishing resorts is desirable; a good boat-landing is to be considered; and last, but not least, when these necessaries of camp are provided for, the camp itself should command a pleasant and attractive view.

We were fortunate in our camp-site in every one of these requisites, except that we did not find the cold spring, but were obliged to resort to a cool stream for drinking water. A stately grove of Norway pines stands on a clear, sandy shore on the east, backed by a thick forest growth. There, about twenty rods north of the inlet from Eighth, we pitched our tent, planted our stove, built our big fire for sociability and our fire in the stove for cooking, and in an hour's time were housekeeping and eating with keenest appetite, and as comfortable as need be. After supper, John took the boat and went off to a point covered with hemlock and soon returned with our bed in the rough, which we quickly, by trimming off the small twigs, converted into a fragrant couch.

The cup of the lad was full. This was "real" camping out. We sat around the evening fire, the elders smoked the peaceful pipe, and told stories under the august trees and the starry night, and then we stretched ourselves side-by-side in the tent for the slumber that seeks tired and happy men. But the boy could hardly sleep for delight. It was his first night in a tent in the woods on a bed of boughs,—and no veteran of camp and tramp in the forest will wonder that the young heart was running over with exhilarant feeling. But finally the hum of the mosquitoes outside of our netting, and the *lap, lap* of the wavelets on the beach lulled us to sleep.

There was, however, a little unaccustomed stretching of limbs, in the morning. There is, indeed, more poetry than softness in a "bed of boughs," viewed by morning light. But a swim in the lake, and a little racing up and down the sand beach in the "original Jacobs" bathing-suit, takes out all the kinks and kranks of a night on the ground; and if there is a stick or stone or knoll not exactly adapted to the curves of the body, it is removed or remedied and forgotten.

The morning discovered to us neighbors. A thin stream

of smoke shot straight up to the sky from the low trees on a point half a mile distant at our left. After breakfast we visited them. They proved to be two young men, mere boys they seemed, from Orange, N. J., who had been fitted out by Jack Shepperd, but had made their way hither from Fourth Lake alone. The marvel was how such young fellows, apparently fresh from school, store or office, carried their boat and did the hard work which seems to require manly strength and trained muscle; but they did it, and were having a most enjoyable time of it. We found them continually referring to " Wallace's Adirondacks " and Ely's map, and with these as their only guides, they were successfully making their way toward Raquette Lake and remoter waters.

If our life at Stickney Camp had been peaceful and restful, this at Seventh was not less so. The sunsets, viewed from the shore in 'ront of our tent, as we looked down the lake and around upon the mountains and forests, were pictures for the painter, and themes for the poet. " Seventh " has been lauded by many an enthusiastic admirer. I should never tire of adding my tribute of praise to its almost peerless beauty, if I did not remember that I have seen so much to admire in the lakes and forests of the Adirondacks that I must reserve something of my enthusiasm for other scenes.

Days too few of perfect weather and pleasant sport and charming life we spent here; and reluctantly but in obedience to programme, one fine morning, we struck camp, packed our luggage and household goods, house and all, went aboard of John's staunch craft, and boldly set out for Raquette Lake; with a firm belief, however, that we should find nothing better in our journeying in the wilderness than the Fulton Chain had proved to be to us.

It remains to be added, before we have said a final adieu to this region, that years ago "John Brown's Tract" and "The Fulton Chain" attracted a large share of the attention of sportsmen and tourists; but that Headley, Murray and others turned the great tide further to the north and east, and for several years, of late, comparatively few, except from Utica, N. Y., have been accustomed to follow the charming old paths into the great wilderness by way of the Moose River waters. As a consequence, much of the pristine excellence of that region has been restored. With all the rest of the well known resorts this has suffered much from the vandalism of tourists and local hunters and fishermen; and something of the grandeur of the more mountainous regions, north and east of it, is wanting. But trout and deer have multiplied as sportsmen have turned their steps elsewhere, and some of the lakes are as beautiful as any in the woods; while there is enough of mountain scenery to continually delight the tourist. One is certain, moreover, not to be jostled by Saratoga trunks, nor to be reminded in these secluded retreats of the whirl and fashion of the outer world which for a season he has fled.

CHAPTER XX.

As a preparation for the hard day's trip from Seventh to Raquette Lake, after our regular breakfast was completed, John had made an enormous pile of pan-cakes for lunch on the way. We were on the water and on our journey at half-past nine o'clock. About a mile up the inlet from Eighth Lake we encountered our first carry of the day, of one mile. Eighth is one of the largest lakes in the Chain, and has mountainous and finely wooded shores, remarkably clear water, and is attractive in every respect. Crossing this lake we came to the formidable carry of evil renown, of a mile and a quarter, from Eighth to "Brown's Tract Inlet" running into Raquette Lake. The day was very warm, our loads heavy, the way somewhat rough, and there was a deal of hard work under a noon-day sun; but I think the carry bears a worse reputation than it deserves. It is a standing rule of guides on "this side" and on "the other side"—West and East sides of the woods—to abuse the passage across the dividing line between the two sections. A sportsman is never advised that it is easy to go over into the rival guides' territory. This unhappy carry, therefore, is berated east and west, right and left, until the traveler in either region is forced to believe that it is not feasible to extend his journey "across the wilderness."

It was one o'clock when we reached the landing on the bank of the Inlet and lunched. John, as usual, after the last mouthful was eaten, fumbled in his pockets for his brier-wood pipe. Alas! it was no where to be found! And he had no other. Every smoker will understand the situation, and appreciate the extent of the calamity. John remembered that at a certain point, half a mile back on the carry, while trudging along under his boat, he had knocked out the ashes from his pipe, but could not for the life of him remember what next happened to the precious thing. We went back over the route, carefully examining every step of the way, stirring up the leaves and bushes, and were returning hopeless from our search, when by good fortune John discovered his pet.

"I vow," said he, as he filled the bowl and lighted the tobacco, "I'll never come into the woods again with only one pipe."

The Inlet is a narrow, deep stream, winding down through a most desolate tamarack swamp, and entering Raquette Lake through a tree-less marsh,—as distressingly desolate a scene as one often comes upon in the wilderness. Sojourners on Raquette are prone to attribute to "John Brown's Tract" the uninviting characteristics of the Inlet; and with this before their eyes and the terrors of the carry dinned into their ears, it is not surprising that they abandon all hope or desire to visit what they conceive to be "John Brown's Swamp."

It was with sensations of exquisite delight that we entered Raquette Lake, renowned and glorious and deserving all its renown. We saw before us a body of water twelve miles in length, with irregular points of land projecting from either side and running far out into it, making a most remarkable configuration of shores. It contains eighteen islands, most of them bold and rocky, and some of them exceedingly beautiful. The lake has, from its size, an open look and a semi-civilized air unlike all the smaller lakes, and very striking to one emerging from dense forests. In sweeping around a point, one almost expects to come upon some quiet town or farm-house on the bay. Take it all in all, it is as magnificent and beautiful a sheet of water as one may ever hope to see in the wilderness. I must add, however, that upon the large lakes the winds sometimes sweep with terrific force and there is danger of wreck in the small boats in common use; and that the fishing pools are so far apart that one often wishes, before the long row is over, that the lake were smaller. I confess a superior liking for the smaller lakes. They are often as beautiful, although not as magnificent, as even Raquette in all its marvel of shores and islands and pellucid water.

We landed at Constable Point, where there is an excellent spring, but the trees have been cut off, and the want of shade makes it undesirable for a warm weather camping-ground; and we went on, across the lake, past Osprey (Murray) Island to the foot of the hill at "Wood's Place," long since deserted, not far north from East Inlet, or Marion River. Here we set up our tabernacle on a grassy spot well shaded by several large trees, near the shore, with good water not far off, and one of the finest views of the lake before us. From the hill behind us, we frequently gazed with unceasing delight upon scenes of forest and lake and sunset which would have inspired an artist or driven him mad at the unapproachable, unreproducible beauty, grandeur and loveliness before him. To the woodsman alone is all this reserved which brush and pencil at best can only faultily suggest. And it is pitiful if the blue-shirted fisherman who camps on such shores and amid such scenes is not also in spirit something of the poet and the artist. Nature is waiting here for the glance of her true-lover's eyes.

In short order,—for we were very tired and hungry,—tent and stove were up, supper agoing, our bed of boughs made, and we were "at home" again. It was surprising, in moving camp, what a genuine home feeling a little cotton cloth in the shape of an A tent gave us, especially when, at the same time, the aroma of the coffee-pot ascended to our nostrils. We also built our "sociable fire" just below the bank near the water's edge, and after supper stretched ourselves on the grass or leaned against the trees near it; and while we watched the sunset, and then the coming out of the stars, and the camp-fires across the lake, we talked over the events of the day and the elders smoked the evening pipe of content and peace. The day had been, on the whole, a rather hard one for us all. John had uncomplainingly borne the heavy loads over the carries and rowed many miles. I had drawn all the drafts on my body that it would honor. And Ned, begging for heavy burdens—

for he was proud to be a genuine woodsman—had bravely borne them, staggering up and down the hills and over roots and logs and bogs. But the fatigue of such labors is easily dispelled in camp. Pure air, plain food and the indescribable something of life in the woods speedily reestablish the disturbed physical equilibrium—for it is purely physical fatigue.

CHAPTER XXI.

The next morning came hot and bright. We visited South Inlet where, under favoring circumstances, there is notable fishing, but we took no fish. While we lounged in the shade, on the rocks at the foot of the rapids, and watched the play of the red-fins with our trailing flies, two parties arrived, on their way to camp at Shedd Lake. One sprucely dressed young fellow had loaded down his boat and guide with camp-kit, brand-new rifle, rods, paraphernalia, impedimenta, luggage and baggage enough for a dozen men. He was a dry-goods clerk from New York,—and this was his first experience in camping. His guide, fraternizing with John, who helped him up the bank with the monstrous pile of stuff, quite profanely characterized "his man" as a "——fool." The other party were old campers, and were quietly on their way across the carry, taking everything at a single trip, long before the Clerk had completed his inventory of his own multitudinous "traps." We learned afterward that his guide traveled all the afternoon, back and forth, and that even then the task of transporting "his man's" baggage was not completed, and they slept at a temporary shelter on the carry.

On our way back to our tent, we called at Chauncey Hathorn's open boarding camp in the pleasant pine grove on the Yellow Sand Beach of South Bay. It is a notable and unique camp, very pleasant, convenient and well conducted by a genuine woodsman who knows how to draw a bead on a deer, write a charming account of it, and to keep a hotel,—a combination of accomplishments which makes it worth the while of the tourist to be his guest, if he does not care for more primitive camping or the responsibilities of forest house-keeping on his own account.

Another day we made an excursion to Forked Lake, passing through the northern and large, open portion of Raquette Lake. We had scarcely got well under way, when a heavy thunderstorm descended upon us in a blinding fury of waters. Pushing for the nearest shore, we landed upon Dog Point (wherefore " Dog" Point, I know not) where, most fortunately, we found an open bark camp, whose occupants were absent. We took possession and lounged and smoked under the goodly shelter until the storm ceased. It is the fashion of the woods for guides and sportsmen to make free use of all camps as they may need, in an emergency, faithfully abstaining from any misuse or abuse. And the hearts of true woodsmen are as open as their bark camps, and their hospitalities as free as the air. A curmudgeon has no business in the woods, but if he has, I think he will shed his shell in a week.

Forked Lake is reached by a short and easy carry, much like a country road. We spent most of the day in alternate sunshine and showers, rowing up the main inlet from the west, where we fished with indifferent success, and also to the north end of the lake. The shores are of singular form, points from either side projecting as if to meet each other, and bays opposite to each other, setting far back into the land. The effect as one passes northward is very surprising and very fine. The entire scenery of the lake, indeed, is very attractive. A single hut or hunter's home, occupied a part of the time by "Captain Parker," a notable character, was the only sign of human habitation or presence. All else was as wild and untamed as Nature made it. When we crossed the carry on our return we found, just arrived, three Poughkeepsie boys, guests of Chauncey Hathorn, on their way to Long Lake. All three, with their luggage and provisions, were in one small boat rather the worse for age and wear. They were without a guide, and the way was new to them all. The wind had risen, they had several times been driven ashore by storms, it was raining and almost night, and they had become somewhat alarmed at the risks they were taking, and wholly dispirited. To add to their discomfort, the fire they were attempting to cook their supper by was principally steam and smoke. It was the forlornest picture imaginable. We gave them our catch of trout and parted from them with serious apprehensions for their safety. However, we learned afterward that young blood, pluck, perseverance and Yankee "faculty" took them through all right.

Our return to camp was against a strong wind and through heavy waves. John was silent, and watched the water intently as he rowed with all his strength and skill. I was anxious and uncomfortable. But the youngster— the Mark Tapley of our party on all occasions—was particularly delighted. However, all's well that ends well. We reached camp safe and sound, untied the tent strings, —the only lock on our cloth house—and the boy and I stretched ourselves out to rest while John prepared the hearty meal which a day's work demanded.

After supper, I saw that John was evidently wanting something besides his pipe.

"What is it, John?"

"Well, you know where you saw a bass jump for your fly, the other day"—

—"And didn't take him, John?"

"That's what's I'm thinking.—that he's waiting to be taken now. If you are not too tired, how would you like to give him another trial?"

"John, I'm not the one to talk of being tired, after such a supper as you have given us; and if you want to, we will go."

"You know," said John, "as I was telling you the other day, that I helped bring the ancestors of these bass over from Booneville to this lake, four years ago. I have never seen a bass caught, and have never eaten one. I'd like right well to do both."

"All right, John;—come on, Ned, you shall have your chance at 'em, too."

The wind had gone down with the declining sun, and the lake was again smooth and gentle. We were speedily on the ground where an evening before I had seen a bass leap. The boy drew first blood and landed his fish. I followed with a little fellow; but evidently the bass of trout waters regarded the proceedings as a violation of the fitness of things, and parted company with us after a brief acquaintance. We started camp-ward, and while passing by moonlight between a certain island and the near-at-hand shore, a fingerling bass, in its flight from an enemy beneath the surface, leaped from the water and struck the boat.

"Hold on, John! I must have a cast here!"

"What! by moonlight?" said John, in surprise.

"Yes, I have taken bass by moonlight when I couldn't see my flies strike the water under the shade of the trees."

I cast, and the fly was taken by a fish that instantly showed his vigor. John watched the bold leaps and play of the bass, untill I finally swung the line around to him, and he took off two bass, one weighing a pound and a quarter, and the other half a pound. That satisfied John, and we hastened on to camp and went to bed, wholly content to sleep without dreams, no matter how pleasant.

When I sleepily opened my eyes in the early morning, and put aside the flap of the tent, I saw John on a broad rock jutting out into the lake, making a careful *post mortem* examination of the stomachs of the bass we had taken the night before. While he cooked them he told me more, I confess, about their food than I, an old bass fisherman, had ever learned from original investigation. As we ate the delicious fellows, I partially forgave John for being a party to the iniquity of stocking these waters with bass, and thus adding one more enemy to the precarious existence of *salmo fontinalis*. That the lake was pretty well stocked was evident from our own experience and that of other fishermen. We saw, caught by others, several bass of about two pounds' weight each. I know that it is disputed that these fish will drive out the trout, but I greatly fear the result of the experiment will be that Raquette Lake will cease to be the home of the gamiest and prettiest fish that swims the water.

From our tent on the beach we could see, across a beautiful stretch of water, the smoke by day and fire by night of a camp opposite. We one day visited this camp, charmingly located among the birches, and found a party of ladies and gentlemen and fine lads, ten in number. Some were swinging in hammocks, reading or sewing; one gentleman was perched, with a book in his hand, on a boulder out in the water; while others, with whom we fraternized, were about the camp-fire, with the guides, talking deer and trout, and watching the preparation of supper. The entire party, with guides, at one time numbered twenty-six, they told me, and their friends were coming and going when they chose, as the encampment was to continue several weeks. They had seen our white tent and camp-fire across the water, and the single boat putting out from shore, and with a glass spied the boy; and they gave us a generous welcome.

Murray's Island is but a few minutes' distance from our camping-ground, and a little to the left of our view in front. Its rocky, bluff shores and heavy forest growth make a pretty picture any day, but as the sun declined, the strong shadows on the water, contrasting with hoary rock and green forest, were something bewildering in their fascination. Occasionally, too, the smoke rose, around the point, above the trees, from the cabin of old Alvah Dunning. He had built his rude hut at the foot of a big tree, at the edge of a clearing where Mr. Murray formerly camped, and cultivated potatoes and a few other vegetables after a very rudimentary fashion. His only companion was his deer-hound. I want to speak very respectfully of Alvah, for he lent us a board for a table; but Ned Buntline thought he was "an old scamp" and drove him out of this part of of the wilderness, a few years ago, by some remarkably close rifle-shooting. When Ned ceased returning to his "Eagle's Nest," Alvah came back again, and now lives his hermit life without fear of the avenging wrath which was kindled by the theft of a boat, committed by somebody.

Of a sunny afternoon, as we lay on the grassy shore, we occasionally saw new parties going to camp at the north end of the lake. The gay flotillas sometimes gave the stars and stripes to the breeze, and as they passed camp after camp, a lusty voice called out in resonant tones for all within hearing, "United States Mail! Letters and papers! Who are you?" Responding to the call with our names, "No mail!" or "Letters!" as the case might be, would be answered back.

Sometimes, parties of two or three came to our landing at the foot of the old and deserted "Wood's Place," to pick berries on the hill, and we had pleasant chats with them. Two young fellows left their gun, which they apparently always took with them, standing by our favorite big tree. The next day they returned for it.

One morning, two ladies rowed over from the camp on Beach's Point with letters to send out, saying that they learned through the guides that we were going to Blue Mountain Lake in a day or two.

After a day of hard work, we took matters very easily the next. On one of these "lazy days," we fished an hour for bass, and then called at two camps on the north side of Long Point—"returning calls," which was not a merely perfunctory performance but a substantial pleasure. One of these camps was in dismay, for there had been a theft committed of a large part of their stores, and a journey to Blue Mountain Lake House was necessary to replenish them.

"Alvah?"

"No; it was a pair of scoundrels that came in by way of Long Lake,—some border ruffians in here on their own account. They know we suspect them and have gone out of the woods faster than they came in." Whether "White" said this or "Smith," I cannot remember.

We had been accustomed daily to leave all our stores and bulky valuables in our tent, merely tying the flaps together in front to signify that we were "not at home," and we felt entirely safe doing so until this incident. The guides are perfectly honest, so far as I ever saw, but some of these border-men who straggle into the woods are of quite another sort.

The other camp, in the thick woods up the hill a few rods from shore, was wholly professional, being occupied by three reverend gentlemen and a lawyer, all in genuine sportsmen's blue and gray shirts. We found them sitting on the ground with their backs to their favorite trees, reading. They dropped their books, greeted us heartily, and gathered around us as they offered us a hillock for a divan, and we chatted pleasantly of college friends of theirs whom I happened to know.

CHAPTER XXII.

The last night before our departure from Raquette Lake, we experienced one of the fiercest of Adirondack storms. The rain, wind, thunder and lightning and dashing of waves were really frightful, in the pitchy darkness of midnight; and I trembled by the hour for the staunchness of cotton cloth and tent-ropes and the firmness of tent-pegs. The force of the storm of both rain and wind was at its highest at about 3 o'clock A. M. I had been awake for a long time, startled almost momentarily by the crash and roll of thunder and the vivid lightning, and the fierce beating of the rain and wind. I more than half expected that at any moment our frail tent would be swept bodily away, leaving us prostrate under our blankets, exposed to the full force of the storm. It seemed as if it would never cease. It raged more and more fiercely. Suddenly, when the rain was dashing in heaviest torrents and at the height of the gale, I heard a snap and a flapping as if a sail had torn loose from the yards, and felt a heavy gust of wind on my face. Throwing off the blankets, I jumped up as if I had heard the yell of a panther at my ear, and rushed to the front end of the tent. A loosely fixed tent-peg at the opening had been drawn, the strings holding the curtains had snapped like threads, and the curtains themselves were flapping and snapping in the wind like a whip-lash. There was imminent danger that our cloth house would "inflate" like a balloon and "go up" and off into the trees behind us. However, I managed to seize the curtains, and shouted to John, who was now as wide awake as I, to light a candle. He took a heavy boot and with the heel drove the tent-peg firmly into its place, we fastened the curtains securely, and then let the tempest howl. We pulled on our boots, to prepare for emergencies, fearing still that the tent would blow away, and crawled under our blankets again. But the gale gradually subsided, and we at length fell asleep.

That was a famously uncomfortable night outside of the tent, but we really suffered nothing inside, except from our fears. Ned did not suffer at all, however, for he regarded the whole affair as "perfectly jolly."

We awoke to find the rain still falling. Breakfast was taken in the tent, with a boat seat on a pail for a table, and our bed for chairs, while John prepared our meal outside as best he could.

"John," said I, as he brought in an extra pile of pancakes, as broad as the frying-pan, "what would you have done, if the tent had blown off last night in the rain?"

"Done? Why, I'd 'ave stood behind a tree and *muled it out* 'till morning!"

We spent the forenoon in "muling it out" in the tent, making up lost time in sleep, studying the guide-book, trying to read a pocket copy of Tennyson, and occasionally dashing out in the rain to catch the signs of the weather.

Finally, at noon, the rain ceased, the wind subsided, the sun came out as serene as Neptune emerges from the waves after a storm; and we resolved to break camp, after dinner, and go to Blue Mountain Lake.

Our stay at Raquette Lake had been very agreeable in many ways. We had seen royalty in the lake itself. The sunset views from the hill behind us were beautiful almost beyond comparison and quite beyond description. We had wandered about, to our heart's delight and content, upon the waters of that and Forked Lake; and we had seen and visited the camps of very pleasant people. But Ned never admits that the Raquette is to be compared with Seventh Lake; and he declares he will never go in the woods again where so many other people go.

Dinner over, we again folded up our tent and stove, packed our blankets and diminishing stores, bade good-bye to the grand old trees under which we had rested in safety and comfort, rowed around to Dunning's landing and delivered over to him the board which had served as our table, and then shaped our course toward the mouth of Marion River, which flows in from the east and is the outlet of Utowana, Eagle and Blue Mountain Lakes.

After a few days upon the large lake, I was glad to be on a river again, near the forest on either side, and sometimes among the lily-pads where the deer had fed the night before, or perhaps that very morning, as we could plainly see. There was a quiet restfulness in the air and the surroundings, a sense of peace and security, a close contact with primitive Nature herself, that were very grateful and satisfying.

There is a single carry of half a mile, much traveled and easy, between Raquette and Utowana lakes—the only one we were obliged to cross that day. The journey through Utowana and Eagle lakes was charming. On the northern shore of the latter, is a comfortable farm-house and a rudely conducted farm of forty or fifty acres. We saw a number of cows feeding in a pasture sloping down to the shore,—a sight which savored so highly of civilization that I involuntarily attempted to adjust my neckerchief, which had wandered around under my woolen shirt collar from one shoulder to the other at its own free will, all the way from Old Forge. We saw Ned Buntline's old home, "The Eagle's Nest," a substantial little house of hewn logs, which stands near the shore and in front of the neat, white farmer's cottage of later growth.

Pushing and winding our narrow way up the shallow and rocky inlet, we entered Blue Mountain Lake, and gazed upon a water view of surpassing loveliness. This, among smaller lakes, is what the Raquette is among the larger. It is three miles long and two wide. Says one author, in endeavoring to convey some idea of its beauty: "Numerous islets and islands of various forms and aspects, some frowning with adamantine sternness, others smiling in robes of charming green, lie in its waters of translucent purity like agates and emeralds in settings of burnished silver. To traverse the winding water-courses formed by these picturesque groups, is to penetrate a labyrinth of intricate and bewildering avenues. The loveliness of the lake is greatly enhanced by the wild and majestic scenery surrounding it. Mountain peaks on three of its sides display their sublime fronts, and preëminent among them is the noble dome from which the lake derives its name."

We quickly crossed the lake, and at about six o'clock ran the prow of our boat upon the sandy beach in front of John Holland's hotel, on the south-east shore, walked up the winding path among the trees, and were again in a house. Ladies and gentlemen, young men and maidens, and merry children were in the parlors and out among the forest trees; while on the broad verandah or piazza, sat and chatted and bantered a number of guides and woodsmen, among whom were "Captain" Calvin Parker of Forked Lake, and the famous Indian guide, modest and faithful old Mitchell Sabbatis from Long Lake,—to be joined an hour later by the redoubtable Alvah Dunning himself.

We had intended to go into camp again here, but there was good promise of rain before morning; it seemed very pleasant and profitable, in its way, to mingle with these original people congregated at the hotel; I was greatly attracted by a good, kind, child-hearted old Doctor of Divinity upon whom I bestowed the entire contents of my medicine chest, carried in my vest-pocket; the seductive influence of a comfortable arm-chair moved me more than it is sportsmanlike to confess; Ned had had about all of the "real thing" that he cared for, although he would not admit it; John was doubly willing to surrender his supremacy as chief-cook; and so we left the tent folded up, and took rooms at the hotel.

After supper, we took a final ride with John out upon the lake, for, on the morrow, we were to part with him; he to return westward, we, in a day or two, to go eastward. The ride was a little melancholy, because it was our last with John, whom both the lad and I had come to warmly regard as a personal friend. He had been as true and faithful as a brother, and so strong and wise and discreet that in all our experience with him, in our long journey and camping, there had not been an accident, mistake or mishap.

The rain came, sure enough, while we were on the lake. We went ashore on an island. John drew his boat on land, turned it over, with one end up on a limb, and we sat and talked the rain out in entire dryness and comfort.

Even Ned confessed to some satisfaction, when we removed our clothing and went to bed in sheets again. But he could hardly sleep. "Do you think we shall ever see John again?" said he. "I never want any other guide but John." Silence for a while;—"How old do you think John is?" more silence;—"Do you think, when I've grown up to be a man and come to the woods, that he will be too old to come with me as my guide?"

But we were tired, and, after our wakeful night in a storm under a tent, very sleepy; and even "John" was at length forgotten in the mysteries of slumber-land.

CHAPTER XXIII.

With the morning, we arose from our couch thoroughly refreshed, not a vestige of fatigue, ache or languor remaining. We sadly shook hands with John, and he started on his long way alone across the lakes, down the winding and lonely streams and over the hard carries, toward Stickney Camp, and on to his home,—only to come back again in a few days, with other sojourners in the wilderness, but not to be "Our John" again, perhaps, for many, many a day, perhaps never. May the years rest lightly on his wise head and on the brave true heart! And may the last "carry" he makes, as he goes to the Unknown Shore, be easy and light, and bring him safe to a good "Camp", where there shall be no night nor storm!

We availed ourselves of an opportunity to make the ascent of Blue Mountain with a party of gentlemen at the hotel, and their guides. The mountain rises nearly 4000 feet above the level of the sea, and is a conspicuous figure in the landscape for many miles, from every direction. We had gazed upon its brow bathed in blue, when on Bald Mountain. We had seen it when out upon Raquette Lake. We had caught glimpses of it on winding streams. It now reared its huge front right above us. The mystery which seemed to dwell on the rugged heights fascinated us the more, the nearer we approached this grand Sphynx of the wilderness.

We made the ascent in an hour and a half, the latter part by a path uncomfortably steep and becoming, near the top of the mountain, a rough stairway of roots and rocks. It would both look and be dangerous if it were not for the trees and bushes which partially hide the roof-like declivity behind you and prevent you from sliding or rolling far if you stumble or make a mis-step. Just where the steepness of the ascent ceases, stands the pine tree up which, on cross-sticks firmly nailed upon it, Kate Field some years ago, and before Colvin's signal station was erected, bravely climbed to obtain a desirable outlook. Passing this point northward, perhaps half a mile or less, along the back bone of the mountain and still rising, (although we found a swampy depression in our path,) we came to a "timber slash" of ten or fifteen acres, where the trees had been felled to give an unobstructed view in every direction. In the midst of this opening, founded upon primeval rock which bears the surveyor's cabalistic characters ineradicably sunk into the solid mass, is erected a tall, steeple-like, skeleton structure of strongly-braced timbers, on the top of which is fastened the signal of bright tin, which can be seen flashing in the sun many miles away, from valley and mountain peak. This is one of the many "signal stations" erected by Verplanck Colvin to aid in his great work of surveying the wilderness by triangulation.

Upon these timbers we climbed, and perching there, twenty feet from the rocks beneath, gazed in every direction upon a wonderful scene. Until then we had never properly conceived of the grandeur of this remarkable region, nor of the "general plan" of the mountains, lakes and rivers of the Adirondack wilderness. It is forest, every where, and mountain, lake and river repeated on every hand; and all these are seen, I imagine, with something of the effect produced upon the mind of the beholder by looking down upon these features of nature from a balloon.

On the south and east, we saw mountains and valleys and the "Indian Clearing," and the silvery, winding courses of Cedar and Indian rivers. At the west, we looked down upon Raquette Lake apparently broken up into half a dozen lakes by the projecting tongues of forest; and beyond, upon Bald Mountain and forest without end. Long Lake and Forked Lake were almost at our feet. Owls Head Mountain, its bald brow bare in the sunlight, seemed not far off; but beyond, the caravan of huge, elephantine backs moved off in procession toward the Canadian line. Turning our gaze to the north-east the grandeur of the scene was almost overwhelming. The true Adirondacks were before us— the almost impenetrable region of mountain heights and gloomy chasms; the region of terrific storms; where mountain peak bellows defiance to mountain peak in the thunders that rock even the mountains in their supernatural force and fury. As far as the eye can reach, this grand mountain range extends,—its gloomy fierceness softened to the eye by the blue haze and the floods of sunshine resting upon the huge backs and shoulders and brows, but made thereby even more shaggy, fierce and terrible to the imagination which defies the air and sun, as haze and sunshine cast their robes over the sleeping patriarchs to hide their awfulness.

Close at hand, too, we looked down into clear and peaceful little ponds and lakes, nestled at the mountain's base in the undisturbed forest, and secure in their insignificance from invasion by sportsman or lumber-fiend, and as beautiful and opalescent as pearls from the Orient.

Our descent from the mountain, quite as trying to the muscles as the ascent, was accomplished in one hour. We lost our trail among the charred trunks of trees where a fire in the dry earth had prostrated several acres of the forest; and we experienced all the woes of a wretched scramble through an indefinitely enlarged brush-heap. Ned and I, however, still had vigor enough to spend an hour after supper in rowing on the lake and winding in and out among the charming islands,—a fitting complement to our day's experience on the mountain top.

Our last day in the wilderness was ended. That night we repacked our bags and bundles; and as we did so, thoughts of work and study, home and domestic life, and of the great, noisy, dusty, busy, fretting and worrying world outside were borne in upon us,—for the next morning we were "going out."

We were called at 5:30 A. M., breakfasted, and at 6:30 o'clock started for North Creek by an "extra," a three-seated "buck-board" stage, which comfortably accommodated five of us besides the locally renowned Mr. Wakely of "Wakely's Dam," who undertook to deliver us at North Creek, the northern terminus of the Adirondack Rail-Road, thirty miles distant, in time for dinner and the 3:30 P. M. train; and he did it—although at the imminent risk and eminent discomfort cf his steeds. Wakely, a man of remarkable force and energy, doubly earned his reputation, that day, as a man to be depended on in an emergency,— but I pitied his horses.

The road for ten miles, through thick woods, was muddy and heavy, (although very good in dry weather,) and we proceeded at the rate of three weary miles every long hour, until we reached Jackson's. For the remaining twenty miles there was a good road through a partially cleared country, winding around among the picturesque mountains, with many hills to climb and descend. The red raspberries, just then in their prime, grew by the road-side in wonderful profusion and excellence. While Wakely was urging his tired horses up the hills we tumbled out and, plunging into the bushes, "ate and ran" in a most ludicrous fashion,—visions of a train departing from one side of North Creek, as we approached on the other, stimulating our pace as we seized a last handful of berries and leaves and ran with all our might to the top of the hill and mounted to our seats without waiting for the horses to stop.

Finally, the little town was reached, the puffing of the locomotive greeted us with an old familiar sound, the veritable North River—the original Hudson—rolled its rapid current at our feet; and our journey "through the wilderness" was completed. There was, however, an interesting rail-road ride to Saratoga, where we took a sleeping car, and woke up at home.

CRANBERRY LAKE

AND

THE OSWEGATCHIE WATERS.

CHAPTER XXIV.

Early in the summer of 1878, there were frequent mysterious gatherings of about a half dozen men of various ages and occupations, in the little back room, upstairs, over Reuben's store on Salina street. Finally, one day early in July, when the pavements were growing hot, a strange collection of bags, boxes, bundles and packages of all sorts appeared in the rear room of the store, and then disappeared by cart for the railroad depot, and away to the north.

On Saturday morning, July 6th, the whole conspiracy, concocted in the little upper room, came out, and the papers got hold of it and duly reported that by the 5:15 train north, that morning, a "lively party" of sportsmen left for a fortnight's sojourn in the "North Woods;" the party consisting of the venerable and genial angler Reuben, whom we had duly made Captain and Commissary, the Senator, the Sheriff, the Mayor, the writer who had been invested with the double office of Treasurer and Scribe, and the Junior,—to be joined at Hermon by the 'Squire, a jolly Justice, both witty in himself and a cause of wit in others.

We had planned to spend two weeks on the Oswegatchie Waters, in St. Lawrence County, making our central camp on the shore of Cranberry Lake, cruising up and down the lake and the Oswegatchie River which passes through it, and visiting adjacent waters if we should find it agreeable to do so.

To the 'Squire, as being "to the manor born" and familiar with men and measures in the region we were about to peacefuly invade, were committed the important details of employing guides, fixing upon the location of our camp—with positive instructions to see to it that an abundant and cold spring bubbled near it—and arranging that transportation should be furnished for ourselves and our rather formidable bags and baggage. As a further precaution against a waste of time and comfort, the Junior, under orders from the Captain, preceded the rest of the party, two or three days, with all the heavy baggage, to prepare a reception in camp for men who expected to be very tired and hungry at the end of a long day of heavy traveling—for we firmly resolved to reach our destination the night of the very day we left home.

We duly assembled at the station and lunched, and the Captain lighted a cigar. At Watertown we breakfasted, and the Commissary smoked a cigar. The Scribe's recollection fails as to the number of railroad changes we made, at each of which there was a anxious gathering up and transfer of rods, rifles and bags and bundles of the smaller sort; but it is a historical fact that none of us were lost or left, and that, on counting the respective noses of the party at DeKalb Junction, there wasn't a vacancy. By stage to Hermon, six miles, was a hot and dusty ride through an unattractive country. The 'Squire was hunted up and found, as busy as a Country Justice could be, at his little office.

Dinner over, at Hermon, the collective Captain and Commissary smoked. We all wrote and mailed our farewells to the vain world behind us, and left our names with the telegraph operator, with explicit instructions to hunt us up whithersoever we should wander; if telegrams came, and to send means to bring us out of the wilderness, all or singly, as the case should require.

The strong vehicle which was to convey us, with the sturdy steeds fresh for the long journey, wheeled up in front of the hotel ; our luggage was deposited therein ; the last things were looked after ;—but the 'Squire had to be hunted up again. He was found, and we all got aboard. But the 'Squire had forgotten his lantern and cigars, and went off in search of them. After some further waiting it was evident he was lost again, and again we hunted him up. He had a faculty of not staying found a great while, all through the trip. Reuben smoked, and a-hemed! He was nervous at the delay. The veteran of many an expedition had learned how precious mid-day moments are.

Finally we were actually all aboard and off, in one jolly load, at 1:20 P. M., bound direct for the foot of Cranberry Lake, thirty-six miles distant. The Captain lighted a fresh cigar as Burnham cracked the whip, and we shouted our good-byes to the assembled village men and boys on the hotel piazza, and rolled dustily out of town forestward.

It was a hot day, the road rough and up and down hill, and it was 6: P. M., when we reached Clarksboro, twenty-two miles from DeKalb Junction and well into the woods.

Horses and men were tired, the dinner of trout and venison was bountiful and good,—and there was something so delicious in the air and scenery of this forest-flanked, mountain-girt and nearly deserted little hamlet, once busy and noisy with the industry of converting the rich ore of this region into iron,—the way to the lake through the dark woods was long and rough,—indeed, there was no help for it, much as we regretted the delay, and we concluded to remain over night, and finish the coming fourteen miles of our journey in the cool, early morning.

Something of the day, and its most comfortable portion, was left to us; and we enjoyed and employed a part of it in strolling about the deserted iron works, and inspecting the large buildings filled with slowly decaying charcoal, the heaps of valuable ore, the *disjecta membra* of heavy and costly machinery, and the falls, on the very brink of which the dam for the iron works had been erected. Here was another of those wrecks of great business enterprises where "somebody blundered,"—the blunder in this case being in forgetting the cost of transporting a ton of iron over a crazy, wooden rail-way out to civilization. The iron is there in abundance and of excellent quality, wood is plenty enough for charcoal to reduce the ore,—but the ruin of the "Clinton Iron Works" tells the rest.

Having all duly philosophized, and lamented the folly of this enterprise, our thoughts turned to more cheerful themes. The Captain lighted his seventeenthly cigar, jointed his rod, and,—followed by us, admiring disciples of the piscatory art as practised well nigh to perfection by our worthy chief,—went down back of the little hotel to the river where it is broad and calm after its plunge over the dam and down the fall. A small, narrow, flat-bottomed boat was secured, into which got the Senator who essayed the oars, and the Captain who was to catch the trout. There was altogether too much weight of dignity in one end of the craft, and weight of body in the other end, for safety. The cockle shell rocked and dipped. The Captain couldn't swim a stroke.

"Take me ashore, Senator!" cried the Captain; "we shall spill out of this thing, certain!"

"Oh, no," said the Senator, taking another hitch on the seat to balance the boat; "we'll be all right in a minute." But, as he said so, in came a hotel pitcher full of water, the Captain issued his most peremptory orders, and the Senator, who doesn't like a wetting himself, shoved back to the shore. Procuring a small, bare-footed boy—a sort of tug to an ocean steamer—the good Captain again duly bestowing himself in the stern of the ticklish craft, with his little spider-like fellow at the oars in place of the Senator, moved beautifully forth, (alas! there was no artist in our company,) casting deftly right and left his choicest flies, all about the pool, under the rocks and trees, up to the very foot of the descending sheet of the river; but cast he ne'er so deftly, not a rise did he get. Still he smoked and still he cast, and lustily now, and gently then, did the small boy ply the oars; and the slowly descending sun winked and wooed, and insects hummed and skimmed and dipped in the dimpling water; but never a trout gladdened the vision of the veteran, and not a break of the surface encouraged us who stood and lounged on the shore and admired and waited and made elaborate jokes. The Commodore (for so we voted him, while the boy defied correct designation) finally furl—reeled in his line, gathered in his unavailing flies and came ashore. There was yet light enough, and we followed him, in a clambering way, to some supposed fishing grounds above the dam among rocks and eddies and pools, where trout ought to have been but were not. They were off, for the hot weather, at the cool spring-holes.

It is not the duty of the Scribe to record here the whispered consultations and conspiracies, that evening, among the well informed of the party, in regard to him of the vocal nose and his allotment in the doubling-up at bedtime made necessary by our limited accommodations.

At four o'clock in the morning we were up, breakfasted as soon as possible, and were off again in good order and excellent spirits, but decorously mindful that it was Sunday morning—a matter which our jovial Captain, in particular, never forgets whether in the woods or out. The cool, fresh, dewy forest and pure, woodsy air were delicious; and the road itself, by day-light, was really quite good. At ten o'clock we reached "The Dam," at the foot of Cranberry Lake, where the Junior, already transformed into a typical woodsman, met us with boats and guides for taking us to camp. However, a small tub of a steam-boat was at the bank, awaiting a party, Chester S. Lord, of the New York *Sun*, and others, who arrived just before us;

and by their kindness we took passage up the lake with them, six or seven miles, and were landed near our already built camp on East Bay. We found three tents erected and fitted up as our bed rooms, a bark store-house for our luggage and supplies, and an open, bark-roofed dining room furnished with a long table of boards. Two camp stoves outside were dimly smoking and prognosticating the combined dinner and supper for which we mightily yearned.

Finally, our hunger appeased, we were in mood to consider our surroundings, while, in a Sunday-like way, we lounged about the tents or strolled by a winding path leisurely down to the water's edge. Our camp was new and clean,—no mean consideration,—in the dense woods, about ten or twelve rods from the water up an easy ascent, and from which, after the intervening underbrush and lower limbs of the trees had been cut away, we looked out upon East Bay and the lake beyond and two or three small islands. A spring of pure, cold water bubbled up between the rocks by the path from which, arriving at camp or departing, it was a luxury to drink whether thirsty or not; while a little way off was another spring, deep and abundant for all the wants of our forest household.

The Lake is about nine miles long, varying from one to perhaps four or five miles in width, and in shape much like a huge, ragged stomach, through which the waters of the beautiful Oswegatchie River pass from the south and on their devious northerly way to the St. Lawrence.

The dam at its foot was built and is maintained to gather water with which to swell the river below, at certain seasons of the year, when logs are to be floated down to the mills in the settlements; and the flow is regulated by blocks placed above each other in a strong, framed sluice-way, and which are put in or hoisted out by machinery, as the water is to be raised or lowered. It makes the lake, in fact, a large reservoir, greatly enlarging it, setting the water back in the streams, into the coves and bays and over the low lands, and everywhere drowning and killing the trees on the flooded lands and along the shore. The ghostly forms of leafless trees, stretching their helpless arms aloft, stand in groups and phalanxes here and there in the wide waters, and a heavy, ugly fringe of like dead trees lines all the shores; while trunks and limbs and uptorn stumps, tossed and ground and woven together by the waves among the standing trees, make a landing exceedingly difficult. In front of our own camp, the labor of two men for a day was necessary to make an opening both safe and ample for our use. The scenery, of course, is seriously impaired. The low descending fringe of green, seen on other lakes coming down to the clear, open water's edge, is here wanting; and the eye grows weary of dead tree-tops and drowned forests. But on nearly every side the grand old hills and mountain brows lift themselves up with coronal fronts of forest green; the bright waters and wavelets gurgle and murmur around the rapid craft of the hunter and the fisherman, and the balm and purity of the perfect air of the forest are here as elsewhere a continual delight.

CHAPTER XXV.

Our first night in the tents was glorious in its slumbers. "Hemlock feathers" for beds, and blankets and mosquito bars made us entirely comfortable; and the deep stillness soothed us more gently than music itself into speedy and utter forgetfulness of all the fatigues of our journey. With the early dawn the Captain emerged from his tent, cigar in mouth, impatient to seize and ply his rod. With stentorian voice he roused the sleepy guides who, not yet having built their own camp, had stretched themselves for the night on the ground about the camp-fire, without bed or blankets. In an instant every man of us was wide awake. That voice of command was new to us. Later in our camping experience it came to our ears and passed as a troubled dream, and we slumbered on until the magic word "breakfast!" was shouted into our tents.

"Up and dressed" is a phrase which means something when only one's coat, hat and boots are removed for the night. A wash basin on a little mound, a piece of soap on a chip, and a towel hung on a limb, a pocket comb, in the morning—and in a twinkling, if breakfast is waiting, the toilet is made. A morning plunge in the lake, and the delicious sensations of the loving touch of a thousand soft and almost intangible arms bearing you up and caressing you, are the reward of early rising, which you may have for the asking when camping in the woods by lake or stream.

The guides were, most of them, young, vigorous, good-hearted and, withal, rather noisy fellows. Our company, all told, now consisted of our party, seven in number, and six hearty guides. Thirteen hungry men to feed, distant from a base of supplies, with a lot of harum-scarum young fellows for cooks, and with a given quantity of groceries, was the problem with which the Commissary grappled and wrestled that morning, with a clear apprehension of other mornings to come, as he went hither and thither, directing, helping and always smoking; and before our two weeks were up the problem floored even him. Figures won't lie, and his were not at fault; but careless waste spoils the most generous mathematical calculations.

The most noted fishing ground near us was "Brandy Brook," a stream of fair size and very cold, coming into the lake from the east, a little north of us, and gathering something of its surprising coldness from Edgar Mountain. To this stream, in two boats, went the Captain, the Senator and the Sheriff. About sixty-five large and beautiful trout were taken; but these gentlemen greatly bewailed the roots, snags, dead limbs and trees that obstructed the stream and made fly-fishing a mournful proceeding. On their return to camp, that evening, the Captain, who is an admirable story-teller and illustrates like a born pantomimist, with great glee related the story of the Senator's **experience.**

The Senator, with light bamboo, and after an honest and gentlemanly fashion, was seeking to entice *salmo fontinalis* with his flies, casting skillfully among limbs and snags, but quite unmindful of what might happen if a trout should seize the line. There was a leap, a turn of the wrist, and the Senator had his fish, a fair sized one, well hooked. The wily trout plunged under roots and snags, wound the leader and flies round and round, in a mazy way, into an inextricable snarl. The rarest skill couldn't save him; and after a little he was free, but triumphantly trailing behind him a portion of the leader and flies.

"Senator," said the Captain, who in another boat had intently watched the contest, "that style of fishing won't do here,—there are too many things lying around loose; when you hook a trout you must just *yank him right out!*"

The Senator had his bamboo and his sportsman's instincts, and they were both alike opposed to this; but the results of gentlemanly fishing were so far all in favor of the party of the second part. In a moment he struck another fish.

"Yank him out! Lay down your rod and yank like blazes!" cried the Captain in great excitement, as he saw what a fine fellow it was that leaped.

The Senator was excited too. He threw down his rod in the boat, seized the line, and hand over hand pulled for dear life and victory.

"Do you call this fishing!" fairly groaned the Senator. A pull—"Blank this style of catching trout!" Pull—"Come out of here! Blank, blank, if I ain't ashamed"—

pull—"of this whole"—pull—"blank business. There! I've got you! but, blank the whole blank business! I feel as if I had been stealing sheep; blank me if I don't! Let's go to camp, Captain,—I don't think I care to fish if you call this fishing!"

The rest of us went up the Big Inlet at the head of the lake, through the floodwood and dead standing trees—at some places very difficult of passage after leaving the main body of the lake—fully nine or ten miles from camp, to the foot of the rapids where the Oswegatchie comes tumbling into the dead water. Not a trout did we take in all that day, although we saw some large fellows leaping in sport. It will not do for the scorner to insinuate that the fault was in the fishermen,—rather let it be laid to proverbial fisherman's luck,—for the Captain and the Sheriff, whose skill needs no vindication, subsequently had there precisely the same experience.

It was the general understanding of the party,—a sort of unwritten law, as binding as the English Constitution,—that the "good places" should be passed around; and by virtue of this law the Mayor and I were permitted to fish Brandy Brook the next day, under a sun that broiled and roasted after a most vigorous and emphatic fashion. The Captain and Sheriff had devoted several hours of faithful labor to removing obstructions, so that there were various open spaces and reaches of water where fly-casting was feasible. We fished as skillfully and devotedly as we knew and with genuine ardor, ascending the flooded portion of the stream to the "quick" water. At the close of the day it was found that I was beaten in the count by one trout. My friend caught one and saved him ; and I had a controversy with a single trout, he on one side of a log and I on the other, in which he came off and got off best. That fish lamented a lacerated mouth, and I a quarter-of-a-pound trout.

CHAPTER XXVI.

All the way from the little upper room to East Bay, we had heard the praises of Grass River sung by members of our party who had been there in former years. Trout were to be had there, large and plentiful, almost for the asking. Lines could be laid in pleasant places, and flies cast in many pools where lurked the eager and gameful fish. The true angler's heart in every one of us yearned for this promised land and its countless wealth of genuine sport. But the way thither involved toil and trouble which even the most ardent sportsman among us dreaded to encounter. The time, however, for decisive action of some sort had come, for the thirteen men of vigorous appetite had consumed the one little trout the second day's fishing had brought to camp, and clamorously asked for more. The fish of Grass River, it was said, were fair,—but it was conceded in the same breath that only the brave deserve the fair. Then it was that the Sheriff and the Scribe arose and declared themselves to be the truly brave men of the party, and stepping out from the hungry ranks volunteered to go forth as a forlorn hope.

On the morning of the third day we set out on our expedition to these happy fishing grounds. Taking with us two excellent guides, Ed. Young and George Sawyer, and provisions for two days, we proceeded down the lake to Thomas's Hotel, three-fourths of a mile above the dam, on the east shore, carried one boat over a quarter of a mile to Silver Lake, as beautiful a little sheet of water as was ever made; and then we safely crossed this lake, four of us and our luggage, bestowed in Young's little Rushton boat 13½ feet long and weighing thirty-eight pounds. We pushed on through the woods to Owens's Plains—an opening where one John Grimshaw, in a forlorn way, cultivates a few sterile acres and tarries to "grow up with the country,"—and struck Grass River at the falls, about two and a half miles from Thomas's. In the woods we were caught in a heavy thunderstorm, but, putting on our rubber coats, we trudged patiently and persistently on,—the only genuinely contented personage of the four being the guide who carried the boat over his head. Crossing the river above the falls on big stones in the river bed, we entered a second growth of spruces so thickly grown and interwoven that we were obliged to cut our way with an axe. Emerging from this, and going on easterly, we at length came to a good woods-road running from the Grass River Reservoir out to Colton, and reached the Reservoir at half-past two o'clock in the afternoon.

Joseph Bolio, a black-eyed, wiry, voluble little Canadian Frenchman of Yankee speech, keeper of the dam, furnished us with a good dinner and his society. Somehow picking up the fact that there was a lawyer in the party, he sought an interpretation of the game law as to killing deer, which might bear favorably upon a "little difficulty" he had had with the authorities, out in the settlements, resulting in his arrest. However, as he had executed a fleet and skillful flank movement just at the nick of time, and was now vigilantly observant of all new comers in his domain, and knew the woods thereabouts and their by-ways and retreats better than any other living man, he was in no special need of any suggestions, of a strictly legal nature, to promote the law's delays, further than to "keep his eye peeled." The Sheriff had to have his little joke smacking of his court room experience, and dryly remarked, "that's the best 'peal for Joe!"

Procuring another boat after dinner, we set out on our journey up the river. Joe thought we might pick up a trout or two in the Reservoir before we came to the flood-wood. Ominous words! but they fell unheeded on our ears, and we jointed our rods and selected our choicest flies —for were we not going up Grass River?

Alas! the water had been drawn low; we speedily reached the flood-wood,—acres and acres of trees, great and small, hemlocks and spruces, torn from the banks above and driven by the rushing waters of the Spring freshets into the basin through which we were to find our way. The surface was nearly covered, but there was a passage somewhere if we could find it. It was so intricate, however, that we often mistook it and were led into places where retreat was the only way out; and we lost much time and strength in wearily forcing our boats in and out among tree-tops, logs and tough, drowned alders. We at length were through the trees, but a worse calamity befell us in the drowned alder swamp, through which we were often compelled to push and pull our way by main force, guided by the slight signs of broken or rubbed limbs where other boats had sometime preceded us, but as often going hap-hazard, on a "bee line," in the general direction up-stream, the perversely crooked channel utterly lost.

Words fail to adequately describe our journeying through this wilderness of difficulties. For nearly four hours we toiled and struggled up the tortuous and uncertain way, hunting for the main channel and often finding ourselves in a "pocket,"—a case of "No Thoroughfare," with no friendly sign-board,—and then backing out or pushing with all our force through acres of dead alders. At length we entered a little stream comparatively free from obstacles. The Sheriff, "who had been there," declared that we had missed the river and were entering a branch from Massawepie Lake. The sagacious guides argued from the "lay of the land" and the character of the woods that this must be the river, while what appeared to the Sheriff to be the river-bed—the entire valley being flooded—was only a bay.

"I tell you again, boys," said the Sheriff, emphatically, "I've been here before, and this isn't the river. We shall bring up in Massawepie, sure, if we keep on."

"Well, Sheriff," I ventured to say, "I have never been here. I don't know Grass River from the Euphrates, by ocular demonstration,—and I'm not likely to, if we don't get out of this everlasting swamp before dark; but I can tell you one thing,—these guides generally know pretty well what they are talking about, when it's a trail or an inlet or an outlet or channel that they are hunting for. Better 'give 'em their head,' Sheriff."

"No,—I've been up Grass River before, and this isn't it, —I'm for turning back and trying another course."

The Sheriff has a host of good traits, and persistence in his opinions is one of them;—but we lost a good hour of day-light in fruitless search of another channel, to gratify him, and at length pushed doubtfully up the narrow stream we had at first entered. Familiar landmarks soon appeared, and then we knew that although well in the woods we were by no means lost.

"Boys, I own up!" at length said the Sheriff, as the truth dawned on his mind. "I'm a culprit of the first water. This is Grass River, and no mistake! I don't believe I know much about the woods after all. If any body insists on ducking me for that extra hour of hard work, I'm ready,—I shan't make any resistance."

The stream was now within its original banks, twisting about as if in pain, and nearly crossing itself in its aimless sauntering down the broad valley. The huge, bare front of "Burnt Rock"—a welcome land-mark—frowned down upon us as we crept by its foot; and at seven o'clock we reached an old bark-shanty, or open camp, which the Sheriff recognized as the one once occupied by him for a noon-day rest. Here we stopped for the night, "as tired as tired could be." We had tried the fishing in the river below at a few points, after reaching clear water, but without success; and our supper, eaten with a keenness of appetite that made it royal, consisted of only coffee, crackers, cheese and onions. We were camping on Grass River, but were troutless!

The guides built a rousing fire, we dried our clothing which was saturated with perspiration from our severe toil, smoked and rubbed on the tar-oil; and the Sheriff and I crawled into "Rat-Hole Camp," (a snug fit for two,) while the tired guides threw down a few boughs on two sides of the fire, (I piled up a few bushes to keep the wind off from them,) pulled on their coats and hats, and lay down to sleep without roof, bed, pillow or blanket.

In the morning, before breakfast, I took a boat and went up the river, fishing on my own account, with a lofty ambition to vindicate the fame of Grass River which had suffered such dire humiliation the day before. At call, I came back with one fingerling. At breakfast we held a council of war. We were right in the heart of that wonderful fishing country which we had heard praised so highly, and the fish were not. The water, we decided, was rapidly going down as the result of drawing off the Reservoir, and if we remained a few hours longer we might have great difficulty in getting out of this inhospitable region; and, further, we were doubly satisfied that the trout had gone somewhere — possibly up-stream, among the alders, in which case we could not reach them, probably down to the flowed lands, where it would be an impossibility to find them. We were forced to the lugubrious conclusion that the drawing off of the water had so changed the conditions that the splendid fishing of the year before, which the Sheriff and Captain had enjoyed, was ruined. This was not an exceptional case, for good fishing changes localities at different seasons of the year, but quite as often at the same season, with more or less water, or with higher or lower temperature. With a trout's powers of locomotion he has a vigorous fancy for making himself comfortable in the best places. Grievously disappointed, and not without expectation of a full chorus of "I told you so!" with variations, from our comrades, when we should again reach them, we reluctantly resolved to turn our prows toward the home-camp.

After concluding our meager breakfast, the Sheriff and his guide pushed on down to Burnt Rock to begin his fishing there, and twenty minutes later, after the water was quiet again, my guide and I dropped slowly down stream while I cast carefully over every foot of water where a trout might lurk. I soon struck a little pool from which I took ten small trout,—all the inhabitants of that place, I imagine,—and then we slowly proceeded until we overtook the Sheriff. I caught but fourteen trout in all, but was elated that I had beaten the Sheriff, my acknowledged superior in angling.

Down stream we went, and through flood-jams, drift-wood and alders, with which we were now painfully familiar, to Bolio's again. While waiting for dinner, we tried our luck in the swift water, eddies and pools in the river below the dam, but without a rise. It is evidently the place of all others for Spring fishing, but July fishing is quite another thing. After dinner another sturdy tramp, and we reached the falls. The water from the Reservoir had raised the river until the stepping stones of the day before were no longer available, and we were boated over the bay below the falls.

Here was the most promising pool for a lusty trout with which my eyes were ever gladdened. The water came tumbling and tearing down the beautiful river among the boulders, and by a sloping fall slid swiftly into the basin below, around which stood large forest trees with thick undergrowth down to the water's edge. It was beautiful in itself, and delightfully enough situated and environed to be, under the surface, a very Garden of Eden for the trout family. I knew better,—but, while waiting for the boat, which the guides had taken across the river above, and off into the woods, before they knew of our inability to cross,—I rigged my rod; and standing upon a shelving rock almost in the middle of the stream, yielded to the temptation which I knew was a delusion, and cast my prettiest and longest. It was of no use. This was not a spring-hole, and no trout in good society would so far forget his position as to remain in town after the first of July, —or admit that he was at home if he was unable to be off at the Summer watering places. The hermit of Owens's Plains told us, however, for our comfort, of marvelous catches in this same pool—"in May."

As we climbed up the river bank and emerged from the forest into the clearing, we were astonished to find the jovial, careless and happy 'Squire, quite at home, talking with Grimshaw and exhibiting a large trout. There he was, in his shirt sleeves, with his rod and his one trout, without coat, blanket, provisions, boat or guide.

"Lost again, 'Squire?"

"No,—I'm here; and what's more, I've got the boss trout,

gentlemen! That's the kind of trout you want to be catching;—it's the kind I take when I actually go a-fishing, myself, and not merely go along for company."

"Well, where on earth did you come from, how did you get here, and where did you get your trout?"

"One thing at a time, gentlemen. I came from Cook's, below the dam. Left there this morning. Fished up the river, and just got here, fifteen minutes ago, waiting for something to turn up. You've turned up, and I'm mighty glad of it, for I'm as hungry as a bear,—I am. Grimshaw has just sent for a drink of water, but I'm afraid of water alone,—I am. Haven't you got something that 'll take the malaria out of it?"

"No,—we don't carry the article;—but, 'Squire, how about the trout—the biggest one we've seen in all these parts?"

"Well, I got him in the river, down here. Big one, isn't he! Oh, he's the boss trout!—that's the kind I catch when I really go a-fishing, I tell you." And he stuck to his story. The "bottom facts" had not then come out, but of those, more anon. It was a fact, however, well enough known in camp, that the 'Squire was the poorest fisherman in the party,—and just how the "boss trout" fell to his lot was the mystery on which we pondered and about which there was expended that night, around the smudge-fire, an unexampled amount of fun and raillery.

Taking the 'Squire in tow, we came on to Thomas's together, procured another boat, and finally reached the home-camp completely exhausted—the Grass River trip ended. The Sheriff, who had been one of the chief singers in the anthems about Grass River, was very unhappy. His song was now a wail. As for me, to return alive was cause enough for rejoicing, and besides, I had seen the worst the wilderness has to offer. But I must add, to be just even to Grass River, that it is the Dam ("with a big, big D,") and the Reservoir that make the region we visited the most desolate I ever saw in the woods; and that the river below the Reservoir is as wildly beautiful as the heart of man can desire.

A night's rest, in the woods as well as out, puts new courage in the heart. The general filling of things that night, on crawling into our tents, seemed very much like sawdust. The next morning, however, everything was glorious again, like the sunshine.

CHAPTER XXVII.

During our absence there had been most persistent and skillful fishing at Brandy Brook, but with "unaccountable misses,"—*a la* Creedmoor. Indeed, that stream was a problem and mystery. Trout of fabulous size leaped and played there daily before the eyes of the eager Captain, but with hardly an exception, after the first day, they refused every proffered fly and bait of every description. The Captain and the Senator, both veterans of the angle and equal to almost any emergency in the art, were hopelessly baffled in all their efforts. They discussed those perverse trout up and down, horizontally and diagonally; recalled and applied all known facts and principles relating to the habits and disposition of the trout family; tried, convicted and duly sentenced them to be caught; and demonstrated each night, before the full council of the camp-fire, that they of necessity must succumb on the morrow to a shrewdly chosen or newly concocted allurement. But each morrow the trout woke up with a new kink of their own, whereby the plans of these valiant fishermen were brought to naught. Reuben might smoke, and smoke, and thunderously "A-hem!" as he nightly pondered over the perversity of Brandy Brook trout; the Senator—as keen in a trout-hunt as in an argument in a law court—might elucidate the principles which, according to undisputed testimony, guide the *salmo* family, and forge a chain of logic which, by all precedents, they could not break; the Sheriff, with grim grit and multitudinous tackle, might hunt them with the detective's relentless vigilance and sagacity; but it was all in vain. Those noble fellows of Brandy Brook leaped and rolled their broad, spotted, shining sides in the sun, and gamboled like lambs on the hill-side; but they refused, with an anchorite's virtue, every tempting offer, flapped their tails at logic, and eluded the stealthy hunt with double the detective's skill. Rarely, to be sure, one was caught, and upon examining his stomach to learn what his royalty fed upon that he had grown so great and so haughtily indifferent, it was found to contain——nothing The Captain, to this day, with a slow and significant shake of the head, maintains that the mysterious conduct of a Brandy Brook trout "beats all!"

But it is comforting to believe that every evil fortune has its compensations. The ill-luck of the Grass River expedition and the tantalizing failures at Brandy Brook gave us both food for wise meditation and a broad and shapely cloud for the silver lining that we were about to behold—besides furnishing a new illustration of proverbial fisherman's luck.

Some of our party had been to the river below the lake and reported, on their return, successes which inspired a general exodus from the home-camp. The next morning after the Grass River experience, five of us, with guides, went down the lake and below the dam for two days' fishing; leaving the Captain and the Sheriff in camp, still unwilling to abandon the contest at Brandy Brook. Three of the five went down the river to Cook's Spring-Hole and several miles further, realizing their fondest hopes. The Mayor and I spent the first day at Basin Brook, a little cold stream putting into the river from the southerly shore, about half a mile below the dam. It is navigable for small boats only about a quarter of a mile, after which it creeps around among the overhanging alders in such a bewildering and contracted way, that in the cool shades and among the holes and springs the trout are entirely safe from even the enterprising small boy and his alder-rod and tow-string. We fished from our boat in a most comfortable fashion, a part of the day, and took out one hundred and five trout, most of them of fair size and giving us excellent sport.

We all spent the night at the house of M. G. Dodds, who is keeper of the dam. He and his pleasant family live a very retired but most sensible life on the river bank near the place of his labors—the rapid river below the bluff making delightful music to go to sleep by. At supper, some very vile slanders were uttered by the Senator and others as to the Scribe's appetite, which he endeavored to render innocuous by intimating that he was both Scribe and Treasurer, and was therefore entitled to double rations. And he bears testimony—and will not be deterred from it by any insinuations, past or future,—that the trout cooked by Mrs. Dodds, and coming smoking-hot upon the table by the platter-full, at stated intervals of about five minutes each, for a whole hour, were the best that he has ever eaten; and he admits, for the purposes, however, of this statement only, that he has eaten an appalling number during the course of his trouting experience.

Bright and early, we were all on the river again. But these were among the days when our friends at home were hopelessly hot and uncomfortable, and the thermometer recklessly reveling among the nineties with aspirations, almost realized, for the tuneful ninety and nine. Even we, in the woods, suffered much this day, and fled from the mid-day sun upon the water to the mossy river banks, and lunched and slept and smoked and slept again, the faithful smudge keeping guard, in the cool shade under the heavy crowned trees. Our catch of trout, therefore, while satisfactory was much smaller than on the day before. During the actual time of fishing, on both days, probably not five minutes elapsed without landing a trout of good size, and I, at least, was satisfied with mere numbers. Like Alexander of old, however, I longed for other worlds to conquer, and hoped before we should leave the woods to take at least one "big, big trout."

While we were fishing near the mouth of the brook, and at the height of our sport, a solitary fisherman in butternut, one of the hangers-on at the Dam, paddled down the river. "Our fun is up, Mayor," remarked I; "that fellow is coming right in here,—no; there he swings, out into the river. He's a gentleman, and no mistake!" And, sure enough, he quietly rowed around to a landing below us, came ashore, and with his formidable tamarack pole and chalkline went several rods above us on the stream and began his fishing. He threshed the water fearfully with his big line and heavy bait, but caught nothing. I was so impressed with the fellow's consideration that I wanted to see him catch something.

"My friend," I called out, "you are not having much luck with bait, are you?"

"No;—guess I've got too big a hook, or something,—they don't seem to care a cent for worms to-day."

"I think I can help you," said I; "if you'll come to the bank here, and throw me your line, I'll give you a fly that the trout seem to like.—There, that brown hackle,—a pretty good sized one, you see,—has been the lucky one for us. I hope it will be for you."

"Thank you, ever so much," the honest fellow replied, as I noosed it on the end of his line and tossed it into the water. That night, at Dodds's, I found he had caught a "good mess" of trout, and I had made a friend. I parted from him with the proud consciousness of having both rewarded and stimulated a virtue.

Saturday night found us all at the home camp again, where we spent a quiet Sunday, the Captain's example and unuttered orders having a most benign effect;—although I am not sure but certain books with feathers and steel in them were conned rather than those for which we owe thanks to the art preservative; and the question was more than once raised, "Have we a tailor among us?" A week of our vacation was gone, and already the shadow of our leave-taking from our sylvan home and the delights of life in the woods was beginning to settle down upon our hearts.

CHAPTER XXVIII.

Our second week of sport opened with a deer-hunt,—which it is allowable to report, since we had only the hunt. We reasoned well, I think, that fishermen should not live by trout and pork alone, but that a little venison now and then is relished by the fishyest of men. Men and guides were sent out upon the lake and ordered to take stations at various designated points of land at which the deer were likely to take to the water. There we awaited the now faint and then rising and swelling notes of the hound, the rustle through the leaves and branches, and the plunge of the fleet deer into the lake. My guide and I waited and lounged on a rock; watched the gulls wheeling about their nests on Gull Island; listened, and heard no sound but the voice of the loon. One by one the boats returned to camp, without a shot. The whimpering and disappointed hound was picked up on the opposite shore of the bay and taken into one of the boats and brought in. And then we planned new ventures for the day.

I had partially engaged with three of our party, successively, to go up the Oswegatchie river, above the lake, for two or three days. But the story of Grass River was too fresh in their minds for the fair consideration of an expedition, the glories of which were vouched for by the word of our guides alone. However, the spirit of the great Alexander still moved me, and I resolved to go at any rate, alone if I must. Selecting Ed. Young, of Fine, as my guide, and taking his little Rushton boat, we set out at 2:30 o'clock P. M. We took tea, crackers, maple sugar, a frying-pan, knives and forks, cups, blankets, a small axe, rods, rifle and shot-gun and matches, depending for the rest on our luck and skill to supply our wants of food and shelter.

Young was a plucky, faithful little fellow, an admirable guide, and knew ever inch of the river we were to visit; so that, having faith in him, it required but little courage to go forth upon the untried waters, and through the strange forest.

Reaching the foot of the rapids, where the river enters the "set back," we concealed our boat in the woods, a few rods from the landing, and clambered up through thickets, over fallen trees, and up and down hills, with our packs on our backs, three miles to Albany Bridge,—a rude affair built of logs, long ago, on one of the old roads through the wilderness. There Young went into the woods, while I, standing upon a rock in the river near the bank, cast over a small pool at the mouth of a brooklet and speedily captured several very lively little trout. Our supper, at least, was assured almost at the outset. In a few moments, Young emerged from the forest with a boat over his head, the counterpart of the one we had concealed below.

The sun was slowly descending, near the end of one of those memorable double-heated days of that summer, as we pushed from shore and paddled up the beautiful river.

Here was virgin wilderness,—no dead trees or flood-wood, and no alders, but the shores coming down with solid step to the water's edge; and the broad-limbed, vigorous forest stretched its leafy arms high above our heads, out over the pure, flowing water. Between enjoyment of the scenery and the shade, and the pleasure of fly-casting, with varying success, over the promising pools and eddies and at the mouths of little streams, the full day-light slipped unconsciously away, and dusk descended like dew upon river and forest.

Suddenly, there appeared in the distance, before my dreamy gaze, the faintest tinge of dull red against the green foliage of the river bank. In a whisper I directed my guide's attention to it, and between us we made out the outlines of a deer standing upon a rock and quietly feeding in the river's edge. I was in the bow of the boat, and my guide sat in the stern plying the paddle. Carefully laying aside my rod, and raising my rifle and bringing it to bear upon the beautiful animal, I kept steady aim while we silently drew nearer,—my guide whispering, "Don't shoot until I give you the word!" The deer went on silently feeding as we gradually approached without being seen, until we were perhaps not more than ten rods distant from him. I grew impatient for the word, but my guide whispered again, "Wait a minute more—we can get closer!" Suddenly, without raising his head to look at us, the deer leaped with a whirl upon the shore like a lightning flash, and plunged into the woods. As he leaped, my guide shouted "Shoot!" And I shot! I never yet had shot a deer with a rifle, on the full run,—and I didn't then. We listened, and in a moment the deer "whistled" sharply, and by that token I knew I had not broken the letter of the law, and the deer that ran away, lived to be shot at another day.

I had enough vain regrets that I didn't "blaze away" on my own judgment of the proper time to fire, although it was not to have been anticipated that a deer would depart without the one, customary, "last lingering look," —and, again, if I had missed a fair, still mark like that, my remorse would have been intolerable, and I never could have told of my loss. As it was, I was comforted by the reflection that I missed a flash of light into which that deer instantly transformed himself. "So much for Buck-ing-ham!"

For the next half hour or so, we hunted up the river for some stray camp for the night, and found one,—the common, open bark-camp, — where we landed at eight o'clock P. M., thoroughly tired and desperately hungry. I had taken more than enough trout for supper, and we were soon rolled up in our blankets, with a roaring fire at our feet, and fast asleep.

The next morning, we breakfasted on trout, crackers and tea, (not so very bad a breakfast, either, if you have a woodsman's appetite,) loaded our small luggage into the boat, and continued our way up the river. We came upon a party of three or four men in camp, lazily smoking around their smouldering fire after (I have no doubt) a somewhat heartier breakfast than we had taken. No introductions are needed in the wilderness, and our chat of a few minutes, as we lay with the bow of our boat thrust into the mossy bank, and as we talked trout and deer, was a pleasant change from the conversational duet my guide and I had kept up all the way from the home-camp.

Mile after mile up the charming Oswegatchie we slowly paddled, keenly enjoying the scenery and the delicious languor of the gratified senses, swaying the slender rod over every promising water with expectant delight, and watching eagerly the flight and gentle descent of the feathery and barbed deception, but scanning at the same time every turn and winding of the narrowing river for a daylight shot at a deer. A singular bush or brush of dingy red was seen ahead of us, slowly crossing the stream, which on closer inspection, proved to be a red fox,—his long, bushy tail floating airly behind him, while his nose just appeared above the water. Now and then a chipmunk or a red squirrel silently paddled his way across the river, his keen, black eyes evidently distressed by the vision we presented to him. The plunge of the muskrat disturbed the silence,—one persistent little fellow swimming rapidly ahead of us with a large bunch of grass in his mouth, for his winter home. Along the bank, we frequently saw the feeding places of the deer; the soft, bare earth by the water's edge trodden like a farm-yard

Little success rewarded our mid-day fishing, but in every thing else this gentle journeying was most enjoyable. At length, between three and four o'clock P. M., about eleven miles above Albany Bridge, at the "Big Flood Wood" where navigation for our tiny craft became difficult, and beyond which were "The Plains,"—those singular, open, treeless regions, natural pastures for deer, found here and there throughout the wilderness, how caused, nobody knows,—we met two gentlemen and their guide coming down the river, returning from an unsuccessful excursion above. We were about twenty-four miles from the home-camp, and deemed it unwise, with our limited time, to proceed further. We turned about, slowly fishing down stream, while our new-found associates pushed rapidly on to their proposed camp, where they invited us to join them at our leisure.

On our way up-stream, my guide had pointed out a noted pool, called "Cage's Spring Hole," at the outlet of Cage's Lake, or Bladder Pond. I had made a few casts without raising a fin. On our return, the sun was a little obscured by clouds and had begun to dip below the tree-tops which cast a mild shadow over the pool. I approached it with the greatest care, resolved that here, if anywhere, I must take my big trout. The main stream, scarcely ten feet wide at that point, came down like the heavy arm of the capital letter "Y," the small, rapid inlet being the lighter arm, and the two forming, at their junction, a deep pool nearly circular, and from forty to fifty feet in diameter.

As soon as we had emerged from the green alders sufficiently to permit casting, my guide checked the boat and held it with his paddle. I threw my best skill into the effort, and laid a fly on the placid water as gently as a mother kisses her sleeping infant. Instantly a half-pounder sprang fiercely at the flies. I nervously struck so hard that, alas! my rod broke. Fish, flies, leader and line went whizzing away. Seizing the slender fragment of my rod in one hand, and manipulating the line with the other, I succeeded in landing the fish. The rod was a new one, hitherto untried, and a poor butt had succumbed. Untangling the snarl, I speedily took and rigged my old rod, tried in many a tussle with bass as well as trout,—a rod that once took twelve bass in five casts,—and was ready again.

Quietly landing upon the point between the streams, with open ground behind me, again I launched the leader and line out over the water; and as the flies settled down, up leaped the trout, two and three at a time. Nearly every cast for a few exciting moments,—they might have been many or few so far as my observation recorded them—brought to basket one or two fish. Finally, tiring of quarter and half-pounders, I put in practice somebody's old precept that "for big fish use large flies."

Searching in my fly-book, I found an outrageously large red-and-white-winged, purple-bodied and tinsel-wound bass-fly, and attached it to the end of my leader, and cast. Julius Cæsar! What a rise! I couldn't help it,—I knew well enough it wasn't "good fishing,"—but I struck as if I had been shot, and sent the fly forty feet behind me in a flash. "Gently, gently!" said I to my beating heart and tingling nerves; and then, with trembling expectancy but with all my skill, laid the big fly right amidst the bubbles left by the mad leap and roll. Again the open jaws and gleaming eyes, the semi-circular leap—and as the trout made an arc on the surface, I struck. I had him! What a magnificent rush!—how the line whizzed and sung through the water! Coming to the surface, he beat the water to a foam, to shake out the stinging hook—as the bass does for the same purpose—but I led him downward to safer depths. Now he tires. Oh, guide, philosopher, friend!—Ed.! my brave boy! handle that landing-net with gentle skill!—wait!—don't hurry—he's off again!—there, now, take him carefully—he can't make another such rush. Yes! there he goes! He has the nine lives of a cat, and the vigor of a mad bull! Careful, now! If you lose him, in you go after him, neck and heels! There, gently, gently! He's safe—he's landed!

Yes, there he lay on the grass, well away from the water's edge, the vermilion and gold of his broad side flashing in the sun-light, a beauty in form and color, and large enough to make the heart of his coat-less and hat-less captor kneeling on the grass by his victim, leap up into his mouth. "How large?" Well—how large?—is that what you would know? Well, if it is size you seek for in fishing, catch a codfish or a catfish, and be happy; but a trout, a genuine brook trout, full of game from tooth to tail, need not be so very large to make an honest angler lose his head with joy at the capture. There was, however, no more fishing until this trout was weighed and measured, and lifted and petted, and turned over upon one side and then on the other, and held up to be looked at, and laid down again at full length; and he measured, under tape line, fifteen and three-quarters inches in length, nine inches around, and weighed, by good honest scales, one and three-quarters pounds. But that which went out of the beautiful form, as it lay gasping on the sod, was the better part of him.

"Did I stop fishing then?" Such is the heart of man,— I did not. The large flies continued to take only the large trout, and when they ceased to allure, the small flies brought out smaller fish. There was some savage work. One frayed leader with its trailing flies yielded to the tug of a mate to my first large trout. Another big-mouthed, sharp-toothed fellow cut the snell of a salmon fly, like a knife-blade. Sometimes defective hooking, over confidence, or eagerness cost me what I thought was a two-pounder. But there had been enough good fortune for the day, and gleeful excitement enough in those two hours to last for a year, and to furnish pleasant recollections for a life time. Finally the trout family went to bed, I said good night to the again quiet pool, and we floated on down the river.

I reeled in my line, put away my flies and unjointed my trusty rod; for there were no more worlds to conquer with that weapon, and if there were, I wanted day-light for the business.

CHAPTER XXIX.

The witching hour of twilight had come, when the timid deer descend the mountains and emerge from the forest to slake their thirst and feed upon the succulent lilypads and tender grasses growing in the coves and bays of the river. While I was seated in the bow of the boat, my guide silently paddled in the stern; and we floated on, winding our way with the tortuous stream, with every sense keenly alive and watchful for the first sign of the presence of a deer. Darkness stealthily descended, and the rifle was laid aside for the long, double-barreled, muzzle-loading, ten-bore shot-gun belonging to one of our guides. A gentle tremor of the boat at length arrested my attention, and my guide whispered, "I think there's a deer in the river, down there; do you see anything?"

"No," I responded, after an eager and prolonged gaze in the direction indicated.

"If you see *anything*, fire at it," said he. But to save my life I couldn't see "anything" but dark shades on the obscured water. Suddenly, as we advanced, there was a splashing and dashing in the river, four or five rods ahead of us, and I saw, apparently, a small, dirty, white handkerchief jerked and switched rapidly about from one side of the shallow river to the other and back again toward the shore where it first appeared, and the dim flashing of water beaten almost to a foam. It happened to strike me as exceedingly comical; but although nearly ready to explode with laughter, I pulled the trigger. An awful roar, as of a park of artillery, burst and rolled down the river and over the forest, shattering the impressive stillness of the night into a thousand echoes. The roar was followed by a silence almost as awful. When everything was hushed again, we listened. The crashing through the trees told of the flight of our game, but it might be wounded; then the noise ceased, in a moment the deer stamped like a sheep and "whistled," and fled away to the mountains.

Re-loading the gun and lighting and adjusting on my head the "jack" that we had borrowed of our prospective hosts, we again silently went on down the windings of the forest-lined or alder-fringed river as before, peering around every point and into every nook and cove, but seeing nothing. Once, we heard a light rustle and delicate footsteps near the river bank, but the thick alders effectually concealed the wary deer,—he stopped, we stopped, each listened for the other, and then he stealthily crept away. Still we threw the light along the banks on our silent way, searching for the two "globes of fire," but saw them not.

At length, at nearly ten o'clock, dreadfully tired and hungry, we reached the camp of our new friends, ate a sumptuous supper provided from their ample supplies and my basket of trout, and then rolling up in my blanket under the bark-roof, while the fire at my feet blazed brightly, I went to sleep forthwith.

Young and Ward, the two guides, however, went out floating for deer. At about 3 A. M. I was awakened by a shot, a dull, heavy, booming sound as of distant thunder, followed by another and a third shot. Fifteen minutes later the boys came back with a yearling doe in their boat, wounded by the first shot, missed by the second and effectually stopped by the third. They had seen and heard eight deer during the night, but the moon had risen and its bright light made it very difficult to approach them.

Our breakfast was good enough for an epicure,—plentiful trout, a large frying-pan full of Bermuda onions, scrambled eggs, coffee, Boston crackers, pickles and minor articles. We rendered great and friendly service to our hosts, who were that day going out of the woods and made it a cardinal point not to carry out with them any of their supplies; and they gave us with their parting blessing something to eke out our much depleted food reserve, which, as the sequel proved, served us a most excellent turn.

The day, July 17, opened with a light south wind which speedily grew stronger, a wicked, red light in the eye of the sun, and fearfully oppressive heat. Proceeding down stream, on reaching Albany Bridge we restored our boat to its original place of concealment, and, packs on our backs, gun and rifle and rods in hand, went down the hard, rough carry to the foot of the rapids, nearly overcome by the heat and thoroughly exhausted. It was two o'clock when we there drew our boat from its hiding place in the bushes and started northward down through the flooded timber.

We both paddled vigorously. The wind, by this time blowing almost a gale, drove us on through the long, open reaches of water at a wonderful and exhilarating rate. We finally worked our way through the two or three specially difficult passes in the flooded timber and driftwood and came to the "fish hawk's nest," a point beyond which the river becomes in fact the lake.

Looking out upon the dark and angry water, we saw that the waves were high and rough. The wind was rushing with terrific fury down from the long level of Dead Creek, and expending its full force upon the long and broad stretch of water we must inevitably descend and cross on our way to the home-camp. The shores were marshes and drowned lands. There was no landing near us where a temporary camp could be made. Our provisions were low. The prospect of a night without shelter, probably in our boat, with a fierce rain-storm brewing, was not agreeable. We were very tired. The next day was to be the last in camp. All these considerations made us really anxious to proceed, despite the forbidding out-look, but we did not intend taking many risks, for we were in no position to redeem a blunder, and could hope for no aid from others in case of disaster.

We approached Dead Creek Bay at its head, in the lee; ventured a little among the waves; scanned the wild, tumbling waters and the mad white-caps; ventured a little further; questioned whether we should try the passage down to the next narrow water, *but continued going as we questioned;* until finally, somewhat to our alarm and quite to our surprise, we found we were in for it and could do no other way than *go ahead*. Our small boat would have swamped in an instant if we had attempted to turn back or change our course.

The wind followed us squarely, and, the further we went into the open water, the harder it blew. My guide sat in the stern and I in the bow, each with a paddle, while our luggage occupied the middle of the little thirty-eight-pound Rushton boat. Young said, "I *think* we'll go through safe,—but don't get scared if water comes into the boat,— it takes a good deal of water to drown a boat!" That certainly, in the circumstances, was encouraging. I answered, through the gale, (in a rather heroic vein, I confess) "Tell me the truth, whatever happens, and what to do, and I'll do it;—I never lose my head in emergencies." That was about all we said, as the wind howled and drove us along up and down and through the hillocks of increasing and foam-crested waves. Never did boatmen handle the paddle with more skill than did Ed. Young, as we tore along through the convulsed and raging waters. There were times when a false stroke would have left us at the mercy of the gale; but the brave, steady-nerved little fellow seemed to have eyes all around his head, and knew the approach of every unusual wave, and how to prevent its burying us as in a deluge. The staunch little craft shook and trembled and quivered, from end to end, under the buffeting of the cruel waters, but responded to Young's paddle as if it had been a part of his body and his nerves ran all along through its delicate frame. There was no Cæsar aboard, to be sure, but the boat seemed to feel the responsibility of the occasion quite as much as did the brave and honest boatman.

We aimed for a green, timbered point, half or three-quarters of a mile below, as being directly in the only course we could go, and the only place (for the dead timber) where a landing seemed possible. After what seemed hours—probably not many minutes—we neared it, our eyes anxiously scanned the ragged, tossing and groaning dead drift-timber for an opening large enough for our boat to run into in safety—and we found just *one* such, which I had observed and remarked upon, in passing a few days before, as being a possible refuge for some poor fellow in a storm. Into this opening we shot the boat to the timber piled on the shore, hauled it out on the stranded driftwood, took out our luggage, placed heavy sticks across the boat to prevent its being blown over upon the sharp prongs of broken limbs—and then, safe at last, and happy to feel solid earth again under our feet, we drew a deep breath of relief and looked thankfully out over the wild and marvelous way we had come.

Our first feeling was of hearty satisfaction that we were ashore anywhere. Our next was a desire to know what awaited us, now that we were ashore. Young, taking the axe, said, "Well, I guess I'll go up here and see what kind of a country we've got into, anyhow!" and plunging into the thicket, disappeared. I sat on a rock and rather dubiously contemplated the tumbling and desolate waters and the more desolate dead swamps and bogs beyond, and the dark, storm-laden sky, while the wind howled and the heaving flood-wood groaned as if in mortal pain.

Young soon returned and said, "There's hard land close by, with plenty of spruces; and we might as well move our stuff up there and fix up, somehow, till this wind goes down,—and may be that's what it will do when the sun goes down or the rain comes. But if it don't, we've got to stay here,—can't tell how long. Anyhow, we shan't starve right off, with plenty of trout and venison in my pack-basket." We carried everything up into the woods, to a pleasant sort of forest-ground, a dozen rods, or so, back from the shore.

"Guess here's a good place to camp," said Young, looking up to see whether any dead trees were likely to fall where we stood. "It's going to rain before long," he added, "and we might as well have a roof, the first thing."

I was completely exhausted, and threw myself upon the ground, quite regardless of rain or any other ill that might befall us,—empty, having eaten nothing since an early breakfast, tired out by the long carry and the paddling, overcome by the heat, and I suppose I must admit that the peril and the excitement had wrought a little upon my nerves.

Young, however, "equal to either fate," proceeded to build an open bark-camp, the growth of which I still had strength enough to watch with interest. He first cut down two small trees, made crotches, and thrust them into the ground six feet apart. Upon these he laid a pole, then four poles upon that and the ground, at the proper angle for a roof. Then he cut and peeled bark from large, smooth spruce-trees,—hacking around the tree near the roots, and then again as high up as he could reach, and cutting a line from top to bottom,—then peeling off the bark with a wedge-like stick, in fact, "skinning" the tree in a moment's time. This bark, in long broad sheets, was laid on the roof-poles, rough side out, shingled and lapped, and set up at the sides, with beveled ends tucked under the roof,—the whole making a snug, perfectly rain-proof camp, open in front, and before which a bright, cheerful fire was speedily built.

Our supper was of crackers or hard biscuits, maple sugar, the hottest of tea, and the tenderest and most delicious broiled venison. Thus refreshed, life became attractive again, although darkness was settling upon us and the wind still roared through the tree-tops, and we heard the grinding and groaning of the flood-wood by the shore, and a tempestuous night was threatened.

Robinson Crusoe and his man Friday (as we very readily imagined ourselves) went down to the shore and watched the waves and coming night, and the white-caps gleaming with the fierceness of the fangs of wild beasts.

Night settled black and boisterous, but we lounged on our bed of boughs in camp before a cheerful blaze, smoked and told stories of other adventures, until, without knowing just when or how it happened, we were abed and asleep. In the night, there was rain which pattered harmlessly on our good roof. Half awake, at one time, I heard stealthy steps on the leaves, and fired a rifle-shot as a reminder that we did not choose to be disturbed by curious intruders. When wholly awake, however, I suspected the noises were made by the mice or rabbits running about where we had scattered crumbs from our supper table on the ground. Some laughter, more stories, and we were asleep again.

The morning opened as calm, and as innocent of evil threat, as a May-day, and the water was like glass. After a hasty and frugal breakfast, we left "Wind Bound Camp," as we christened our temporary home, loaded our luggage, launched our good, staunch little craft, and speedily paddled our way of seven miles to the home-camp, where we were heartily greeted and congratulated by our party, who had had not a little anxiety on our behalf—and our excursion up the Oswegatchie was ended.

Letters and papers in good quantity, by the hands of some incoming party, had arrived in our absence; we learned that the outer world was conducting itself quite properly without us; and thus reassured, we were full of satisfaction, and prepared to enjoy to the utmost the few remaining hours of our abode in the wilderness.

CHAPTER XXX.

As this was to be our last day in the woods, we were all content to do but little hard work. Brandy Brook, the usual resort when nothing better offered,—still enticing to the Captain, the Senator and the Sheriff, because of the mysterious conduct of its large and comely trout,—was visited by several of the party and with the usual success. The Mayor and I, with the strong and willing George Sawyer as our boatman, went up Chair Rock Creek, to see a colony of blue herons and their remarkable nests. Of these latter there were thirteen in the dead, drowned trees, built of sticks and mud, generally upon the top of a high stub, like a saucer on the head of a cane. The birds themselves, of a bluish gray color, with their small, slim bodies and long, thin necks and legs, looked like the dead limbs of the nests and the surrounding trees that they sat on, (a fact freely offered to Darwin); and they had a way of standing up in their nests, like sentinels, and, when shot at, slowly sinking down until they were invisible. A lucky shot with a "Stevens' Pocket Rifle"—a wonderful little weapon with ten-inch barrel, and of twenty-two calibre—at a distance of fifteen or eighteen rods, brought one of these birds from its perch near its nest, a hundred feet from the ground, to the water in which the tree was standing. It came down with a tremendous thump and splash, dead. It measured, from tip to tip of its wings, five and a half feet, and, from beak to toes, four and a half feet. It was a vile smelling wretch, and after being duly inspected at camp nobody had the slightest desire to bring it home as a specimen for the taxidermist's skill.

But the crowning event of the day occurred in the morning. The Junior and the 'Squire, with a guide, took a boat and left camp for the dam. In a few moments we were all startled by a shot and then a yelling as of a dozen savages. We rushed pell-mell down to the landing.

"Hurrah! Man over-board! Hurrah! Hurrah!! Man over-r-r-board!"

It was the lusty voice of the 'Squire. His arms were beating the air like mad. Seizing the small American flag, which had heretofore fluttered in the breeze at the landing, he waved that as he shouted, again and again; and the boat was returning to shore. The real hero of the occasion (and the same wasn't the 'Squire) sat quietly in the stern of the boat, his broad-brimmed, drab hat drawn modestly down, and his hand in the water. As they slowly approached, there were many speculations as to the occasion of this great uproar of the 'Squire's—a matter, it must be explained, of no unusual occurrence, as he exploded after this fashion on the slightest provocation, especially if there was any fun on hand. The boat, at length, entered the opening through the flood-wood and approached our primitive dock, and the mystery was solved; and a pair of buck horns appeared above the surface, firmly grasped by the Junior,—the body of the animal being submerged.

After the general hurrahing and congratulations were over, it came out that after the boat had proceeded a few rods from the landing, the deer was seen leisurely swimming out into the lake. Chase was given. The deer, discovering his pursuers, endeavored to return to the shore, but his retreat was cut off by quickly rowing the boat between him and land, and then he dashed wildly out to sea. The Junior aimed carefully at the head of the animal, and fired with fatal effect. Before the deer could sink, the boat was shot swiftly to his side, the Junior seized the antlers,—and the rest we had seen. We all rejoiced that it was the good fortune of the Junior, as genial and modest a sportsman as ever drew a bead or cast a fly, to carry off the laurels—and the antlers, the latter of which with the beautiful head and neck now adorn his office on ——— street.

The next morning, July 19th, after an early breakfast, we broke camp and started for home. A pang shot through our hearts, as the tents came down and collapsed into cloth,—houses and homes and sanctuaries of refuge from rain and mosquitoes, no more,—only bundles of cloth, to be packed and lugged and stowed away, for a whole year, until summer heats again should drive us out of the torrid city into the cool forests and beside the clear waters of the great wilderness. Our camping ground looked desolate, after our luggage had all been taken to the landing, and as we went back, ostensibly "to see if we had left anything," but actually to silently and half sadly say good-bye to "Camp Reuben."

Our loaded boats moved gaily down the lake to the dam. The inevitable "settling the bills" was accomplished;

Burnham was on hand, by appointment, with a Concord coach drawn by four horses, and a large open wagon; without unnecessary delay, we shook hands all around with the Dodds family, whom we all remember with pleasure and gratitude, and with our guides, most of whom were good fellows; shouted and sang our farewells to Cranberry Lake, with a cheer and a "tiger" for the Brandy Brook trout, with "ways that are dark and tricks that are vain"; and rolled and bumped and thumped away, over the corduroy of the first mile, and the roots and stones and hills succeeding, toward the outer world.

As we approached Cook's Spring-Hole, the Senator, who enjoys that sort of thing, for the hundredth time began to quiz the 'Squire about his "big trout."

"'Squire," said he, "come now! Tell us just how you caught your big trout. Do you mean to insist, now that we are going out of the woods, and must all begin to get back to the habit of telling the truth,—do you mean to stick to it that you caught that trout with a hook and line?"

"Gentlemen," said the 'Squire—and he had the air of a stump orator every time he opened his jolly mouth—"Gentlemen, I have told you a hundred times that I caught that trout in Cook's Spring-Hole, with hook and line—and that is true"—

"Yes, yes," chimed in all the rest, "that's what you've told us, *that's true*—but honest Indian, now, you know."

"Well, gentlemen, we'll ask Cook himself;—there he is, up by his patch of corn."

"Yes, we'll ask Cook, but you shan't bribe him, 'Squire, with that black bottle,—down with it!"

"Gentlemen," responded the 'Squire, as he lifted aloft the bottle, "I shall appeal to Cook to tell the truth, the whole truth and nothing but the truth!—Here, Cook!"— we had driven up to him, and the stage had stopped,— "here, Cook, didn't I catch that boss trout with a hook and line?—Here, take a drink before you speak,"—handing him the bottle—"you can tell the truth better with the taste of this in your mouth."

"Shame, shame! 'Squire, to bribe the witness!" cried the Senator;—"Cook, isn't it the honest fact that the 'Squire caught the trout in a net, and didn't you see him do it?"

Cook had taken one good, long drink, and was handing the bottle back to the 'Squire, his eyes longingly following it, and his lips smacking.

"Tell the truth, Cook," said the 'Squire; "didn't I take it with hook and line?—Here, before you answer, take the rest of this!" handing him the bottle again.

Cook took it, held it up, and with his eye measured the contents.

"Oh, take it all, Cook," said the 'Squire.

Another look,—there was enough spirit in the bottle to send him into a fence-corner for the rest of the day,—and he said, "*I guess old biler'll stand it!*" and swallowed the entire contents.

"There, now, Cook—tell us the truth—didn't I catch that trout with hook and line?"

We listened to see what answer was coming, after two such drinks;—it was given deliberately—

"Well—*I didn't see you catch it any other way!*"

The Squire shouted, "Gentlemen! I'm vindicated! Drive on, Burnham!—Good-bye, Cook!"

But—within an hour, we had brought the 'Squire to the confessional—and he admitted that the "boss trout" which the Sheriff and I saw him so proudly bearing at Owens's Plains, was caught by Cook in Cook's Spring-Hole, the night before, with a net—and that he bought it of Cook!— We were approaching civilization,—and the truth-telling instinct of the civilized man was moving the 'Squire. We never heard, however, what became of Cook's "biler."

We reached Hermon in the evening, re-organized our outer man, and once more enjoyed the luxury of clean sheets. Early the next morning, we looked for the 'Squire to say good-bye,—but he was lost again; and as we rolled out of town, in the stage, a sadly humorous refrain, without rhyme or metre, might have been heard above the rumble of the wheels, conveying to the attentive listener the information—"Oh, the jolly, jolly 'Squire,—he's lost again, —he's lost! lost!! lost!!!"

In due time we reached our homes, and were resolved into our original elements as humble citizens, with, however, something of the forest, the tent, the mosquito-smudge, tar-oil, and Cranberry Lake clinging to us still.

A few "general observations," and I relieve the reader who has followed thus far the fortunes of the Cranberry Lake party.

The weather in the woods was unusually warm, but we had no "realizing sense" of the terrible heat outside, until we reached Hermon and the newspapers.

Cranberry Lake, itself, is not a good body of water to camp on. It is too large, being easily moved by the wind, and so made dangerous on many days when a smaller lake would be safe; and too much time and labor are required to visit the various fishing resorts, of which it has no more than many a small lake,—certainly but few spring-holes where trout must be sought in July. Its shores, lined with dead wood, standing and fallen, and its bays and flooded swamps often impenetrable, are both dangerous to approach and exceedingly disagreeable to the eye. On the other hand, the lake affords a large and safe breeding and feeding ground for trout, and will long be noted, I imagine, for its many and large fish.

One ought to camp above or below the lake, on the Oswegatchie River, thus having really attractive scenery, easier and safer moving about, and equally as good and probably much better fishing.

The river below the dam is rapid for half a mile, and the finest place, all things considered, for Spring fishing in the woods,—a comfortable home with Dodds, at reasonable rates, not being the least consideration. In Basin Brook, within a mile of the dam, in a single pool not over twelve or fifteen feet in diameter, the Mayor and I, while floating quietly, with faces near the water, saw at least half a bushel of trout, some of them from fifteen to eighteen inches long. At Cook's Spring-Hole, about five miles below the dam, there is probably the best fly-fishing in all that region. There are, also, several other excellent spring-holes in that immediate neighborhood.

The river above the lake, after two miles of rapids, is navigable for small boats, without a carry, for fifteen or twenty miles, and has fine spring-holes—"Cage's Spring-Hole" probably being the best. The Spring fishing, on and above the rapids, is said to be admirable, and the river here is much resorted to by sportsmen from the adjacent towns. Albany Bridge, three miles above the head of the river, is the point of entrance to the river above the rapids and the region above the lake, a tolerable road leading from the rail-road at Governeur to Fine and then to the Bridge.

The upper Oswegatchie River is also a remarkable resort for deer; and I saw the banks of the stream, at several points, trodden like a sheep-yard, and many well beaten deer-paths leading to the water. I do not know a section of the wilderness where the experience of the guides, Young and Ward, of seeing and hearing eight deer in a single evening's floating, would be likely to be repeated.

Undoubtedly, both the Oswegatchie and Grass rivers, at the proper season, and when the water is at the right height, afford as fine trout-fishing, both as to number and size of fish, as any other part of the northern wilderness.

But the genuine sportsman, the true lover of forest, lake and river, the tired brain-worker, the seeker for health and recreation, each desires, in his brief forest-life, more than fishing and hunting. The grand and beautiful scenery, the quiet and lonely lakes and streams, the mountain heights and secluded vales, the silvery waters in all their variety, and the endless charm of the ever young and ever old forest, all contribute of their richness abundantly to those who have eyes to see and hearts to enjoy.

CHAPTER XXXI.

No serious work, like the present, is complete without at least one didactic chapter. The opportune moment and page have arrived, when and where I propose to give some hints and suggestions, which old campers are requested to omit as not being needed by them, but which all neophytes are invited to read.

The term "Adirondacks," in popular use is applied to that north-eastern portion of the State of New York which is still almost an unbroken wilderness, and being parts of the counties of St. Lawrence, Franklin, Clinton, Essex, Warren, Hamilton, Herkimer and Lewis. Across this wilderness, east and west, the distance is about eighty miles,—north and south, about one hundred miles. It has a wonderful water-system of lakes and rivers which enables the adventurer to explore its innermost recesses; while the mountains, in ranges and groups, are grand and majestic.

The entire region is skirted by rail-roads distant from its borders about ten to twenty-five miles, the intervening space gradually shading off into primitive forest. These rail-roads are, on the south, the N. Y. C. and H. R. R. R. from Schenectady to Utica; on the west, the Utica and Black River R. R. to Carthage and Philadelphia, and the Rome, Watertown and Ogdensburg R. R. from Philadelphia to Potsdam Junction; on the north, the Vermont

Central R. R. from Potsdam Junction to Mooer's and on to Rouse's Point; on the east, the Delaware and Hudson Canal Co. R. R. lines from Mooer's southerly to Plattsburg and on to Whitehall, and through Saratoga to Schenectady. From Saratoga the Adirondack R. R. runs north-westerly fifty one miles to North Creek, aproaching the forest directly on the route to Blue Mountain Lake.

There are twenty or thirty reasonably good entrances to the wilderness from these rail-roads, and the principal ones —following the same order—are as follows:

From the N. Y. C. R. R. at Amsterdam, Fonda, Little Falls and Herkimer, to Lake Pleasant, Round Lake and Piseco Lake—the route from Fonda by rail-road to Gloversville and thence by stage to Sageville being the easiest and best.

Entering from the Black River R. R. and connecting roads on the west, stop at Remsen for Piseco Lake region, and Jock's Lake; at Alder Creek, for Woodhull and Bisby Lakes; at Booneville, for Moose River waters, Fulton Chain, etc., and through by Raquette Lake; at Lowville, for Beaver River waters, Fenton's or "No. 4," Beaver Lake, Albany Lake, Smith's Lake, and through by Tupper Lakes; at Governeur, for the upper Oswegatchie River, above Cranberry Lake, and Cranberry Lake; at DeKalb Junction, for the lower Oswegatchie River (below Cranberry Lake) and Cranberry Lake, the usual route to the Lake; at Potsdam, for Raquette River and the lakes flowing into it.

Entering from the Vermont Central R. R., on the north, stop at Malone for Meacham Lake, "Paul Smith's" on St. Regis Lake, the Saranac Lakes and through the wilderness in every direction,—a most popular and much traveled route; at Chateaugay, for the Chateaugay Lakes.

From the Delaware and Hudson Canal Co. R. R. lines on the East, enter at Plattsburg by Railroad to Point of Rocks, thence by stage to "Paul Smith's" on St Regis Lake, or Martin's on Lower Saranac Lake, and on at pleasure to any part of the wilderness; at Port Kent, (Lake or Railroad,) by stage to Keeseville, Point of Rocks, and then as last above; at Westport, for Elizabethtown, Keene, Keene's Flats, through the Adirondack Mountains proper, to North Elba, and on to Saranac Lake. At Saratoga, take Adirondack Railroad for Schroon Lake, or to its terminus at North Creek for Blue Mountain Lake, Raquette Lake and on through to any point in the Eastern and Northern wilderness, or from North Creek north to Adirondack Iron Works, Lower and Upper.

With the aid of an ordinary map of the wilderness the foregoing information will enable the tourist to form the plan of almost any tour he may desire to make in that region.

The sportsman will need to consult works designed to point out more specifically the best resorts for hunting and fishing. However, the guides in any of these localities can give complete information, and the hotel keepers, at nearly all these points of entrance, may be relied upon to post the inquiring sportsman. "Wallace's Guide to the Adirondacks," is exceedingly valuable in this connection.

Where to go and *how* to go into the Adirondacks, depends principally upon whether you go as a *tourist* or as a *sportsman*,—whether you wish to journey, or to camp. If you go as a tourist, you should select some of the easier routes, and those upon which regular conveyances run,—as, by way of the Adirondack Railroad and stage to Blue Mt. Lake, or by rail-road to Point of Rocks and stage to Paul Smith's. However, conveyances for parties of three or four or more can be procured at reasonable rates at any of the points of entrance already mentioned.

Again, as a tourist you may take your family with you. There are, on the principal routes through the wilderness, comfortable although generally unpretentious "hotels," less than a hard day's journey apart, so that an entire family, including ladies and children, may travel for a hundred miles and sleep under a roof every night.

For such a journey, gentlemen may wear their ordinary clothing, being careful, however, to provide boots or shoes suitable for occasional muddy walking over "carries," a hat that will endure a smart rain, and a light rubber overcoat. Ladies need good walking shoes, dresses that do not trail, and rubber wraps. A good umbrella is serviceable against sun and rain. Woolen clothing is best. On the water, *sit still in the boat*, heed the suggestions of your boatman, and you are as safe as in a rail-road car. Leave all heavy baggage at the point of entrance, or have it forwarded to the point where you are again to resume rail-road travel.

As a sportsman, seeking the wilderness for the fishing and hunting, the requirements are very different. First, to find fish or game, you must go to solitary and secluded lakes and streams, away from the much-traveled routes;

and you must camp, and be accompanied by guides; and sufficient provisions must be taken to supply your wants for the number composing your party and for the time you propose to remain in camp.

For clothing, wear no linen; take your last cast-off woolen suit, a woolen shirt with collar of same material on it, a soft hat, strong (but not very heavy) boots or shoes, a woolen blanket and rubber overcoat. Wear woolen or merino socks. Carry a few needles, some strong thread, and buttons of various sizes. A strip of adhesive plaster, a small bottle of brandy, and a piece of Turkish rhubarb, (decidedly necessary with most persons the first few days in the woods,) are all that are ordinarily necessary in the medicine-chest.

For sporting, one fly-rod, one bait-rod, with extra tips for each, lines, reels, hooks, leaders, and a small assortment of flies of medium size, are an outfit for fishing; and for shooting, take a double-barrelled shot-gun for night-shooting or a rifle for day-shooting. Better than either, and combining both, is Baker's three-barrelled gun—two shot and one rifle—the true arm for the Adirondack sportsman.

For camping, the guides will easily build or find an open bark-camp before which a blazing fire burns nightly. A tent is warmer, cleaner, and permits you to move from place to place more freely. An "A" tent of cotton cloth, water-proofed, 7 × 8 feet on the ground, weighs about ten pounds and is good for three. Through the top, sew a rope extending 15 feet each way, use crotches outside of the tent and pegs to tie to, and you can dispense with the annoyance and burden of tent-poles. A camp stove is a great comfort and convenience but not indispensable. Duncklee's is the best in market. A better one is built to fold up much like an envelope, made at cost of less than $5, and weighing less than ten pounds, but there is none such in market. My own, of this kind, is a complete success. To acompany this, get a large, strong tin-pail, with cover, and put inside a smaller tin-pail with cover. Inside of this, put coffee-pot, tin-plates, cups, knives, forks, spoons, a frying-pan with detachable handle, and dish-cloths. The coffee-pot must have a bale, and the frying-pan should be of good size, if you have no stove. However, most of the guides furnish cooking utensils. Ask some old camper to make a list of "supplies" for you, if you do not already know what you want.

If you seek the Spring fishing, go in May, as soon as the snow is out of the woods, and fish on rapids and in swift water. Fish with bait, generally, at that season.

If you care more for the delights of camping, and want to enjoy forest life, and also want fly-fishing, go in July or August. July, on the whole, is the most delightful, and the safest month for settled weather. At this season, look for trout in the "spring-holes,"—it is a waste of time to seek them in the rapids or deep water, or in the body of a stream. Look for them at a spring or pool of cold water. Find where a small cold stream enters a lake or river. Whenever you find clear *cold* water you ought to find trout.

Early in the season, the dreaded black fly abounds, but he departs by the middle of July. The mosquito and midge or "punky" come before July, and stay. None of these, however, are a serious inconvenience if "tar-oil," camphor and lard, or some other of the well known mixtures for warding off insects are persistently used. Insects rarely accompany their victims out upon open water. A breezy camp, also, is pretty free from them. Mosquito-netting at night is worth all the trouble it costs to arrange it.

In camp, hemlock or balsam boughs, and plenty of them, make the best bed. Each person should have a blanket to himself, and roll up in it. Wear a soft hat, cap, or other protection on the head. Take a small flour-sack and fill it with hemlock twigs or grass and put a coat over it for a pillow.

Have plenty of jokes, but no "fooling" with the axe, the boat, or with each other, in camp or on the water. Bodily injuries or a dead man in the woods, with long "carries" on the way out to civilization, are great inconveniences. Few people become sick in the woods, and, with care, accidents of a serious nature are not likely to occur. Of all things, avoid going off into the woods alone, away from the water or the trail. Nothing is easier than to "get lost," —nothing much harder than to "get found" again.

Guides usually charge $2.50 or $3.00 each per day, including boat. Hotels usually charge 50 cents each for meals and lodging, or from $7. to $10 per week for board, with use of boats. In camp, the food of each man costs not to exceed 25 cents per day. One guide and boat for two sportsmen is comfortable,—a guide and boat for each sportsman is a luxury worth paying for if you can afford it.

One guide and two boats for a party of four who are willing to work, and with a fixed camp, will give all the substantial benefits of a sojourn in the woods.

Finally, don't fish all the while,—enjoy the woods, the waters, the camp-fire, *everything* including the hardships, and bring away all the bright, clear-cut memories you can of a region unsurpassed for its glorious combination of rare sport, beauty and grandeur.

Grayling Fishing

IN

NORTHERN MICHIGAN.

CHAPTER XXXII.

In the summer of 1879, on my way home from a western business trip, I was able, under the most pleasant auspices, to gratify a long cherished desire to visit the haunts of the Grayling in the Northern Wilderness of Michigan. The result of various letters and telegrams was, that on a Monday morning, July 21st., an excellent friend of mine, of Detroit, and I, found ourselves together in that goodly city, planning the details of our week's vacation.

Law, politics and public duties had so engrossed my friend's time and affections that he lacked one thing sadly, —he knew absolutely nothing about fishing. But he had the true disciple's spirit, and, with becoming humility, besought me to "rig him out" for the woods and the rivers. A serviceable fly-rod, from Mr. Long's stock, and the necessary accompaniments from my own abundant supply furnished him in good style as a fisherman.

We telegraphed M. S. Hartwick, hotel proprietor at Grayling, Crawford County, on the head waters of the Au Sable,—"Provide men and boats for two, Tuesday, noon train." That evening, we proceeded by rail to Bay City, and on the following morning resumed our journey to Grayling, thirty-five miles further north. From Bay City we passed through a flat, wooded, and exceedingly uninteresting country. Occasionally, however, from the car window, we saw some very pretty little emerald lakes, which had a half-wild, half-mild beauty that contrasted strangely with the surroundings. The rail-road pushes up northward, past station after station, where once were a steam saw-mill, a collection of rude cabins, a "hotel" and a "store," and where now the mill is going to decay or is burned down, the cabins deserted, and the whole town consists of a forlorn family or two. The valuable pine of the neighborhood has all been cut, sawed and marketed, and the town experiences "reversion." The railroad presses on to new fields, and the history of the lower lumber regions repeats itself. At some points, however, the soil shows itself susceptible to cultivation, and a sparse farming community springs up. So much we saw on our way to the village of Grayling. We saw much that was better and more promising, in the northern part of the Peninsula.

Hartwick, our host, had complied with our request, and engaged for us the services of two good men. One of them, William D. Jones, is a famous fisherman, hunter and trapper, who knows all about Northern Michigan, its rivers, lakes, fish and game. Within three years he had trapped forty-two bears, shot many deer, and fished for grayling in the Au Sable, Manistee, Cheboygan and Pigeon rivers. The other, Charlie Robinson, served us well, and "poled" to our entire satisfaction.

· By the middle of the afternoon we had procured our supplies, blankets, etc., and then we took to the river, close to town,—the Au Sable, famous in the recent history of grayling fishing in this country as, perhaps, the finest grayling stream in Michigan. At this point it is not more than twenty feet wide and has an average depth of about one foot, with holes and shallows interspersed, and with crooks, snags and rapids that necessitate a peculiar boat and method of propulsion.

We had two boats, flat-bottomed, with sides nearly perpendicular, pointed at each end, and having a "fish-well" or water-tight compartment, about one-third the length of the boat back from the bow. The water-tightness was relieved, and the box made available for keeping fish alive in it, by pulling half a dozen plugs from auger holes in the enclosed bottom of the boat. The cover of the box made a comfortable seat for the fisherman sitting face bow-wards, while a round, old-fashioned "cat-hole" in the seat, on either side, invited him to plump in his fish as fast as taken, —they being supplied with fresh water from the river, through the auger holes, in a degree of abundance corresponding with the avoirdupois of the man above their prison. Fat anglers are the grayling's favorites;—fatness means water, and water means life.

The boatman, or "poler," as he is locally known, sits or stands—as the ease or difficulty of his work permits or requires—in the stern of the boat, in a contracted space that suggests an easy loss of equilibrium and a consequent ducking. Armed with a slender but tough-fibred pole, which is about ten feet long and pointed at both ends with iron, he forces the boat rapidly along the shallow stream, around the sharp curves, among the snags and through the rapids,—or checks it in the swiftest current, to afford a cast over a promising bit of water,—with consummate skill. It looks simple enough, but a trial of this easy thing, by a new hand, demonstrates that there is science even in poling a flat-boat in swift water, down-stream.

It quite often demonstrates how cold the waters of the Au Sable are. (I shall not say what befell my friend, who was of an investigating and experimenting turn of mind—and who weighs well nigh two hundred pounds.) In the occasional stretches of deep and quiet water—the "Still-water"—the iron-shod pole is laid aside (then look out for your rod and flies if lying by your side!) and the paddle comes in play.

The Au Sable "runs down hill" with a gliding, sliding motion at the rate of four miles an hour. Poling up stream with empty boats is possible but not feasible,—with a load, well nigh impossible; and fishing parties arrange "to be called for" at a designated point down the river, on an appointed day, and to be drawn out, boats, bag and baggage, on a lumber wagon, to the rail-road station.

After the river leaves Grayling, it gradually increases in width to fifty feet or more, with a variable depth from six inches in the broad rapids to two or three feet,—its average and natural depth being, in July, about eighteen inches. I only speak of it as I saw it for about nineteen miles. Below, it becomes a broad, strong river. The "sweepers," or fallen trees across the stream, have been cut out of the Au Sable, for a long distance, depriving its passage of much of its pristine excitement and adventure. We saw enough to enable us to comprehend the situation of a boat swiftly descending the rapids around a point and coming suddenly upon a prostrate mammoth cedar, all bristling with sharp, dead limbs—right across the water highway, at just the most inconvenient height above the stream. The old college problem—what would be the result if an irresistible force should strike an immovable object?—hardly suggests a more disagreeable predicament.

On either side of the river a belt of heavy timber grows, partially because fed by the moisture of the stream, percolating through the soil, and partly because the ground is "bottom lands." The higher ground, rising back from the river, so far as I saw, is mainly sandy soil and partially covered by a scanty growth of stunted jack-pine. A depression in the surface, gathering and confining the rainfall, produces a heavy growth of timber.

Down the wood-fringed, embowered aisle of the Au Sable we were at length swiftly gliding, under the tutelary care and vigorous poling of our two boatmen. For six or seven miles there was no fishing, and we had ample time and opportunity to observe the beauties of the charming river, winding gracefully and rapidly down its course; its cold, clear waters revealing the sandy bottom; the air pure, fresh and invigorating.

At length, the word was given,—"there are grayling here!" I made my first cast. In a flash, with a leap out of water, a fish seized the fly before it touched the surface, and was fairly hooked, with scarcely an effort of mine. I hastily drew him in—he weighed only four ounces—and, for the first time, beheld the marvelous colors of the large dorsal fin and the pectoral fins, the silvery sides, the olive-brown back, the "V" shaped black specks, (where the trout has the crimson spots,) and the graceful, taper form of the grayling. If I had not taken another fish, I should have felt repaid for my journey. Pages of description had not given me the whole agreeable truth about this beautiful fish, that was revealed to me in the two minutes' examination I gave to this "specimen number," before I plumped him into the well.

Casting again, I struck a fine fellow that showed great vigor and activity for two or three minutes, and despite Charlie's urgent appeals to "land him," I gave him full play and studied his form, colors and spirited movements in the clear water, as he passed up and down, within twenty feet of the boat. The magnificent dorsal fin, erect like a warrior's plume, waved like a battle standard, and glowed like a rainbow, and his shining sides flashed in the sunlight like silver. It was, indeed, a beautiful sight, and I enjoyed it to the full before he finally succumbed and lay panting on the surface. When I finally drew him in, he weighed ten ounces, measured thirteen and one-half inches in length and six and one half around,—a slender fish, as these measurments show, but typical of all the grayling I saw. In some rivers, I was told, they are thicker than this, but everywhere more slender than trout.

The evening was now approaching; and, after taking another pair of grayling, we hastened on to West's Landing, where we camped for the night. The guides made a tent of blankets, a fine bed of balsam boughs, and concocted a good supper of the fish we had taken, flanked by many things from our hotel. I tried to believe that the grayling is as good to eat as the trout, but yielded only a modified assent.

After breakfast, the next morning, while our men were doing the house-work of our tabernacle on the Au Sable, my friend and I walked back from the river, half a mile through a wooded belt along the river bottom, to the elevated plateau where the scraggly jack-pines prevailed, scattered and small, and to a farm which Mr. West had initiated on the poor, sandy soil. On our way back to camp, we surprised a large and very fat hedge-hog that waddled off into the underbrush, his slow movements, as he shambled along, being notably accelerated by several innocent and harmless sticks cast ineffectually after him.

Putting everything aboard our boats, and interchanging boatmen, (by which arrangement Jones fell to me,) we proceeded down the river, fishing as we went. The early day was delightful, not too warm although bright and clear, but afterward becoming cloudy. Later, the clouds became heavy and dark, an east wind blew smartly up-stream, and at length some rain fell, but not enough to drive us to shelter.

We fished for five miles down the river to the "Hay Road," where we dined on shore. During the morning I had taken twenty-one grayling, throwing back two of that number because small,—all kept alive in the well.

In the afternoon, I fished one and a half miles further down stream, and back again to the Hay Road, until five o'clock P. M., capturing twelve grayling,—my entire catch for the day being thirty-three, and for the day and the evening before, thirty-seven. Of these, three weighed ten ounces each, and measured as I have described my second fish. Quite a number weighed half a pound, or a trifle more. They were a glorious sight in the well, when I landed and gazed at them to my heart's content, before permitting the men to despoil their fair forms.

My prettiest sport was had at a deep, narrow and swift passage in the river, up which we were forcing our way by clinging to the branches and working as best we could. Jones held the boat right in the edge of this swift water, while I cast up-stream, taking fairly large fish frequently. One ten-ounce fish, struck in the water above me, rushed swiftly down stream, forty or fifty feet below the boat, before I could check him. At the instant, when I brought him to bay, he sprang fully three feet out of water,—as magnificent a leap as I ever saw,—flapping his tail with a noise that I distinctly heard above the rush of the rapids, as if applauding himself for his gallant exploit.

"Gracious!" said I.

"Gosh all Christopher!" said Jones.

I wouldn't have missed landing that fish, after such a display of his beauty and strength, and after the brave battle he made for the next five minutes, for the best bamboo ever won at a fly-casting tournament by either of those veterans of the angle, Reub. Wood or Seth Green.

The team met us at the Hay Road, at six o'clock P. M., and we tediously drove fifteen miles through the jack-pines, the heavy timber, and finally over a corduroy road through a swamp, back, late in the evening, to Grayling and our hotel.

CHAPTER XXXIII.

"What I know" about grayling and grayling streams (in addition to diligent reading on the subject) consists only of what I saw during these two days, and of what I learned by persistently interviewing our boatmen, other fishermen wherever I found them during our trip, and from the "local authorities" on fishing. But such information as I picked up, I believe to be accurate and reliable, and worth repeating for the benefit of the lovers of good sport. Sifting it, I give the results, as follows:

I.—GRAYLING STREAMS IN NORTHERN MICHIGAN.

The Au Sable, running eastward to Lake Huron. This, perhaps, is the most widely known of the Michigan grayling streams, and as a consequence, has been over-fished. From a point six miles below Grayling to Big Flood Wood in Iosco County, there is, with exceptions, grayling fishing:—*ordinary*, down to South Branch; *fair and better*, between South Branch and North Branch (except in stillwater for three miles below South Branch); *excellent*, in Big Creek which comes in from the south, about five miles below North Branch, and being, by the windings of the river, about fifty miles from Grayling. There is very little stillwater in the Au Sable, that of three miles between South

Branch and North Branch, and another stretch of six miles from a point two miles below North Branch to Ball's Bridge, near Big Creek, being substantially all, in the fifty miles. I learned very little of the river beyond Big Creek —that being the most distant point ordinarily visited.

Manistee. The upper waters of the Manistee, where the grayling of that stream are now chiefly found, are easily reached by a good road from Grayling, of eight miles. The fishing extends with decreasing excellence, down to the rail-road, near Walton. The Manistee empties into Lake Michigan.

Cheboygan. This river runs northward. Its upper waters are reached from Gaylord (a rail-road town, twenty-eight miles north of Grayling) by a drive of from ten to twenty-five miles. It has not been much fished, and its grayling are reported to be larger and more abundant than in any other stream in Michigan.

Pigeon River, another northern stream, is highly spoken of, but I obtained no definite information about it.

For a trip, limited in time and easy to make, the Au Sable and Manistee rivers offer the best inducements to the fisherman; but, doubtless, there is finer sport as well as harder work on the Cheboygan. All these streams were originally extremely difficult of passage, on account of the "sweepers" and snags. Since the grayling has come to favorable notice some of the rivers have been "cut out" and rendered easy of descent, notably the Au Sable and the Manistee. The Jordan has ceased to be a grayling stream,—the popular verdict being that the trout have driven out their less belligerent cousins.

II.—HABITS OF GRAYLING—SIZE—FLIES TO USE, ETC.

Grayling, in a general way, have the habits of trout in similar streams. They are found in rapids, in deep scooped-out holes with sandy bottom, both in the channel and in the margin of the streams; seek shaded places and spring-holes; and lurk under and near old logs, if the water is rapid, and under over-hanging trees. (I took eight, besides pricking two or three more, in a few minutes, in a hole under an over-hanging cedar.) If the water is rapid just above a hole with sandy bottom, and a tree projects over it, grayling are almost certain to be there. Deep and rapid water in the middle of the stream is also a favorite resort. They are not to be found in still-water, at any time of the year, except that they seek their spawning beds, in the Spring, in the sandy bottoms of quiet water just below and as near as possible to rapids. As the water grows warmer, they go upon the swift-water and stay there during the remainder of the warm season. They never go up very small streams,—being in this respect wholly unlike trout.

Grayling "travel" but little,—seeking their homes for the Summer and remaining there. If frightened out of them, they speedily return when the danger is past. A hole once fished out is fished out for the Summer. They are very peaceable, both among themselves and with other fish, and do not drive each other out of favorite places.

As to size, I heard of grayling being caught in Cheboygan river, weighing two pounds. In the Au Sable, the largest caught in 1879, up to the date we were there, was eighteen inches long and weighing one pound and eight ounces. A pound grayling, measuring fifteen inches, was taken by a party which we met at the hotel. One of seventeen inches in length weighed one pound and seven ounces. The average weight of 950 fish taken by the party was one-third of a pound each.

I am indebted to Mr. Jefferson Wiley, of Detroit, Mich., for a copy of the fishing record (which I give below) made by the company referred to, as well as for much other valuable information about grayling and their capture.

RECORD, SIX DAYS' GRAYLING FISHING.

1879, July	16	17	18	19	20	21	6 days
Rev. Dr. Rexford	12	25	56	44	22	23	182
Mrs. Rexford	6	14	9	27	13	6	75
Mr. Tomlinson	20	42	47	30	47	32	218
Mr Newcomb	11	38	31	29	35	43	187
Mr. Wiley	55	30	43	93	32	35	288
Totals	104	149	186	223	149	139	950

Mr. Wiley was the only expert fisherman of the number, and they all fished with moderation.

Grayling take the fly with great eagerness when feeding, but, like trout, sometimes "play" about the lure in frolicsome leaps. When in earnest, they rush and leap with all the vigor and quickness of the trout, seize the fly almost unerringly and firmly, hooking themselves. They respond to the first cast or two; and, if they miss, jump two or three times, even when near the boat, before abandoning the pursuit. They take the fly almost equally well above the water, on the surface, or beneath it; but my own observation led me to think the last is their favorite method.

When hooked, they make a vigorous rush, and seek to run under logs and brush. If the water is cold and the fish in best condition, it leaps two or three times like a bass, *lashing its sides with its tail.* The fish of the Manistee, which is a very cold stream, almost invariably leap out of water when struck, while those in the Au Sable, not so cold, generally do not.

The appearance of the grayling in the water, when hooked and excited and struggling, is something beautiful to see,—the large dorsal fin being the most conspicuous and noticeable feature. The colors of both the dorsal and pectoral fins are rich and delicate beyond description,—the violet, pearly and golden tints and rainbow hues, marvelously contrasted and blended. The back is dark olive-brown; the sides and belly, silvery; the body, slim and graceful; the head small, mouth of medium size and tender; tail, forked and broad; and the adipose fin shows his royal lineage.

The grayling is a spirited fighter, for a few minutes, but he does not seem to me to have the "bottom" of the trout, nor to display quite the trout's savagery.

When taken fresh from the water and cooked, the meat of the grayling is firm and the flavor delicious; but I must still think the trout bears off the palm for excellence.

Flies for grayling fishing should be of medium size— between a large and very small trout-fly. Large flies "scare the fish." Brown-hackle is called the best,—the grizzly-king, good. The local fishermen say, "Avoid bright red in your flies;" but Mr. Wiley had fine success with the red fly. A good trout-cast of small flies is well adapted to grayling fishing. Change the cast only for dark and light days (bright flies for dark days); make no change for seasons.

Handling the rod in this fishing differs in no respect from casting for trout, except that it is sometimes well to let the flies sink two or three inches in the water, and there is less necessity for the alert "strike;" while it must be remembered that the grayling has a tender mouth.

He is a simple, unsophisticated fish, not wily, but shy and timorous. He is a "free biter," and is bound to disappear before the multitude of rods waved over his devoted head. The sport he affords in his capture, the taste he gratifies in the frying-pan, and the allurements of the charming streams he inhabits, all conspire with his simplicity to destroy him. Could he but learn wisdom from his crimson-spotted cousin, and would the sportsman have pity on this beautiful and gentle creature of the smoothly gliding rivers, he would long live to wave the banner of beauty and glory in the cold, clear streams of the North. But that cannot be.

CHAPTER XXXIV.

We took the noon train, northward, to Gaylord, the northern terminus of the Jackson, Saginaw and Lansing R. R. There procuring a team, we were conveyed directly across the wilderness, twelve miles westward, to Elmira, through a heavy forest of beach, maple and hemlock. We saw many incipient pleasant homes and future rich farms on the way, chopped and hewn out in the heart of the wilderness. Elmira is a town consisting of a single house in the woods, on the Grand Rapids and Indiana R. R. We flagged up a train and took passage to Petoskey, on Little Traverse Bay. This is a wonderfully bright little town, five or six years old, "beautiful for situation," whence one may gaze out over the blue waters of the charming Bay, and upon the distant and broader waters of Lake Michigan beyond,—and dream of peace without heat, dust, or discomfort of any sort but a crowded hotel.

"Bay View," a mile north, is a famous camping ground of the Methodist Episcopal Church of the West, and is the favorite summer resort of thousands of people of all denominations.

Taking an early morning train, we retraced our way to Boyne Falls, proceeding thence through the woods six miles by stage over a good road to Boyne, a hamlet at the head of the North Arm of Pine Lake. The Boyne river, one of the celebrated trout streams of Northern Michigan, enters the lake here. It is not over twenty or thirty feet wide, but is "cut out" for six miles, affording extended fishing grounds notwithstanding its proportions. The trout of this stream are said to be larger than in the Jordan, which enters the South Arm of the same lake. They have, however, a partiality for bait, and there is little or no success with the fly. We wanted to try these waters, but could not devote to it the rainy morning which befell us.

A. J. Hall, a genuine woodsman, intelligent, active and good-hearted, keeps a small hotel at Boyne, and attends to the wants of fishermen. We afterwards had special occasion to remember him kindly.

Taking passage on a little steamer that plies the waters of Pine Lake, we enjoyed a two hours' ride to the quaint old town of Charlevoix, that stands perched on the high bank of the short river emptying Pine Lake into Lake Michigan. After dinner we engaged a boatman,—a bright-looking young fellow, who haughtily bore the distinction of being the favorite "poler" of A. B. Turner, of Grand Rapids, the most celebrated angler of Michigan. We felt sure he was the best man for us in all that country,—but we were as verdant and anserine in our judgment as the "poler" was lazy, mendacious, and generally worthless. The truth was, as we learned later, that he frequently needed a good ducking—which Turner, on occasion, was entirely willing and able to give him. I am happy to add that he does not live in Charlevoix. I have respect for that bit of antiquity.

With boat and man on board, we steamed away, with charming scenery near us on either shore, to the head of South Arm, and were soon rowing up the Jordan against a strong current, toward the promised land. The river, after a brief progress up-stream, became too rapid for the use of oars, and the iron-pointed pole was brought into requisition. The stream strongly resembles the Au Sable,—the clear, and cold water, the swift-gliding current, the heavy-wooded banks and over-hanging trees, all seeming to have been mysteriously transported from the river in the east to the westward flowing stream.

Our advance was slow and difficult, and it was night-fall when we gladly disembarked, five miles up the river, and walked half a mile inland to the rustic forest-home of John B. Webster. There we were comfortably entertained for the night, and also found a pleasant party of fishermen from Akron, Ohio, with whom we forthwith fraternized.

The following morning we entered with spirit upon the trout-fishing of the single day which we had allowed ourselves on the Jordan. Going up the river a mile and a half, our poler declared we were at the head of the good fishing, and pointed the boat down stream and held it fast. That was the proper moment for Jeff's ducking! The truth was not in him,—the best fishing was above us; but so was the hard poling. Our ignorance, however, was blissful as yet, and it is pleasant to remember that for a brief season we enjoyed the delusion.

The day was exceedingly bright and warm. The trout that could not have seen our every motion, for double the length of a cast, would not have been worth the taking. The stream had been daily whipped and threshed, from its mouth to the still blockaded region above, from the opening day of Spring-fishing until this 25th of July, by thronging fishermen from all parts of the country. The trout left in that watery highway were as well educated in all the "arts and wiles" as the gamins dodging about among the legs of men and horse's feet in the crowded city street.

I rigged my fly-rod with special care, adjusting a most killing cast of flies.

"You can't catch anything with the fly, now," said Jeff.; "June is the time for that."

"Oh, well, Jeff., we'll try a hand,—it's too bad to come so far to fish with worms, you know."

"That line is too large," said Jeff., giving my oiled silk a most contemptuous glance.

"Very well," I replied, "here's one" producing another reel and line ready for any emergency, "and this, certainly, is small enough."

"Perhaps so," continued Jeff., with a dubious air, "but that's no sort of a reel for this work;—and your rod is too limpsy;—your flies ain't the right size or color. I tell you, you can't get trout with the fly now—June's the time.— That sort of casting won't do for trout, either,—you won't never get one at that rate."

I was proudly doing my very finest work, and the comments of this wise poler—"Turner's favorite"—were not pleasant but grievous. It was now certainly about time for Jeff.'s ducking! I considered the matter,—but the longer I considered, the more I thought my need of Jeff. was greater than Jeff.'s need of me,—and I "took it out" mainly in biting my lips and wishing Jeff.'s nose would snap up my tail-fly, just in the nick of a vigorous cast of the line, without, however, involving me in any moral responsibility. I should have "played" him with a gentleness and compassion only equalled in tenderness by that of good old Izaak Walton when he sewed up the frog's mouth. It is true, I said something—that was human nature—but only "words! words!"

When Jeff. had been in a measure reduced to silence and subordination, we proceeded again with our fishing, my friend with bait and I with flies. Here and there we picked up a trout, the modest fly and humble worm in friendly contest, and neither gaining a lead worth boasting of. Jeff. was answered, however, for the fly did take trout, the "Impsy" rod brought them to basket,—and it wasn't June, either. Changing from fly to bait and back again, I had about equal fortune with each. But the day was against us, the best hours of the late afternoon were lost in returning over troutless waters to the steamer; and we brought away more delightful memories of the river itself than we did of its famous swift-flashing trout. It is a glorious stream (I was not blinded to that) and I have no doubt it deserves all the high praise it has received. Everybody told us, however, that it had been over-run all summer and "fished to death." It is every year fished more and more, —and so will pass away the glory of the Jordan.

The steamer was in waiting. Jeff., the unmitigated, and

his boat were got aboard, and we followed. Arriving at Charlevoix, we found the hotel full to overflowing, but were comfortably cared for at a cleanly boarding house.

When the next morning came the church bell rang, but likewise blew the whistle of the little steamer "Clara Belle," which was loaded with the rustics of Boyne, South Arm, Jordan and the scattered homes and hamlets in the woods,—off for an excursion to the Island of Mackinaw. To "kill time," or "make time?"—that was the question. On due consideration, we choose the latter, and went on board with the excursionists and pursued our appointed journey.

If it were not such an old, old wonder and beauty, it might be worth while to attempt to describe that perfect day, with the blue, dancing waters beneath, and the blue, deep and serene sky above; the green forests crowding down to the sandy shore; the pure air,—dustless, odorless and noiseless,—fanning the cheek in gentlest breezes. The people of the Middle West have found the secret of healthful enjoyment on their magnificent lakes. When summer heats come down with blighting and enervating effect, the excursion steamers, bearing family groups and merry parties of friends, speed away to the North. On the dancing waves of grand old Superior, along the cool, forest-clad shores, far from carking care and thronging men and withering heat, these Wise Men of the West gather and garner new vigor, and bear homeward with them pictures of marvelous beauty and memories of happiest days.

The rustic people with whom we were thrown, this day, were an honest, quiet company. The women rather plainly showed, in their sallow faces and angular forms, the care and hardships of pioneer life and long, northern winters. The men, although more robust and of healthier countenance, were yet thinner and less buoyant in spirit than a similar party in the East.

A melodeon, placed on board for the occasion, discoursed music at frequent intervals, while the people listened in a solemn way. Quiet, neighborly visiting among the older people, and harmless flirtations between the modest young people, were in progress all over the boat. At length, lunch time came, and numerous baskets were produced on deck, which turned out an enormous quantity of toothsome edibles. No basket was more bountiful in good things than that of A. J. Hall, the inn-keeper of Boyne. Our hungry eyes (tell-tale exponents of something else) opened his generous heart, and we were feasted as liberally as if we too were from the woods of the Boyne or the Jordan.

The Michigan shore was, all along, plainly visible on our right, but at length, almost imperceptibly rising above the waves on the north, like a summer cloud the Northern Peninsula appeared. Our course had been, so far, almost north, but now swerving eastward we sought the passage through the Straits of Mackinaw. Historic places were pointed out to strangers, the narrowing channel brought the wild shores near us for inspection and admiration, and in the distance rose the rocky heights and precipitous shores of the Island of Mackinaw itself, on whose crowning point stands the fort and where waved the American flag.

The outlines grew sharper, the rocks towered higher, as we approached. We swung into the harbor, neared the dock, and in a moment more stepped on shore among the hackmen, the loiterers and the summer visitors who had come down from the hotels. Wending our way to the John Jacob Astor House, we found our friends of the Jordan, who had kindly gathered up our mail at various points and gave it to us here.

We learned that in two hours the good steamer, the *Marine City*, was due from the Sault de St. Marie ("the Soo") whither it had gone with a Detroit excursion party. We resolved to "keep moving" toward home by every opportunity, and to take this steamer that evening for Detroit. The interval between our arrival and that of the steamer we employed in rambling about the quaint, peaceful, dreamy town, strolling along the shores, and clambering among the rocks by the water's edge to Arch Rock—a "natural bridge" which has been described and pictured so often that I only stop to say it did not "meet expectations."

We had time to catch the spirit of this strange old town of the North, sitting a queen where the fleets of the inland seas float east and west through the narrow way at her feet, and pause to pay homage. It seemed the Castle of Indolence of the cold North where the Vikings might rest in peace and content after wars and bloodshed,—rather, the summer home of the old Thunder-God, Thor himself, where the wild winds would murmur him to sleep. Better, it is indeed the resting place of the weary men of the South, where the purest air, the serenest days, the most serious scenery, and the far off, dreamy gaze over the waves will lull and soothe and restore the worn mind and the tired heart. It was with reluctance—almost with sadness—that we gazed our too early farewell to the historic and romantic island, while we stood on the upper deck and the steamer moved silently out upon the darkening waters and into the evening shades,—the steamer's band, meanwhile, discoursing strains of music tranquilizing, tender, and soft as the ambient air or the mirror-like waters beneath. The long, quiet evening on the water followed. We sat on the upper deck in easy chairs, and talked of the streams and woods, of old college days together, of the homes and home-ones we were journeying toward, of those we shall see no more on this side of the River, of—but we were two old friends, boys together once, "old boys" now,—and it is ours to remember what we talked.—It was late, very late, when we went to our state-rooms.

All night long the good vessel plowed her way through the silvery waters, trembling through every fibre with her eager ardor. All day long she moved with the superb strength born of fire and steel and vapor. She halted at the coast towns to take on and discharge passengers and freight; the band beguiled the waiting-time, and we tramped up and down the streets until the whistle sounded a return. The wind came up fresh. I remember how easily and with an airy grace quite exquisite, my Mackinaw hat lifted from my head and sailed off into the Huron to commit *felo de se*—the sixth suicide of the sort on the steamer's trip.

The sunset, that evening, was matchless in beauty, but grew terrific to see and feel. The angry orb wrapped himself in tinted clouds which he dyed in blood. As the darkness came down, thunders crashed and rattled through all the air. Lightnings smote downward from the sky into the black, heaving bosom of the water, like the avenging sword of an archangel. Winds shrieked and howled among the ropes and chains like affrighted spirits of evil. Then came the dash and pour and din of the torrents of rain,— the blackness of darkness, impenetrable to the eye save by the frequent lightning shafts, adding its horrid majesty to the scene. It was, altogether, something fearful and grand; and the tales that were whispered, of wreck and disaster on these stormy waters, lent additional gloom to the night and tempest.

However, all that passed, and the morning came in peace and beauty, as if summer sun never grew angry and summer skies never frowned nor grew black in the face. Through the St. Clair, with its suggestions of fishing and duck-shooting, and down the Detroit River, with charming resorts along its banks, we glided on our way. The last good dinner on the *Marine City* was hastily eaten. We rose from the table, gathered up our slender luggage, walked over the gang-plank, and were in Detroit. There we separated,—our week in the Northern Wilderness of Michigan ended.

THE END.

www.ingramcontent.com/pod-product-compliance
Lightning Source LLC
Chambersburg PA
CBHW030748250426
43672CB00028B/1365